## ABOUT THE AUTHOR

**Norma Walton** is a partner in the law firm of Walton Advocates, Barristers & Solicitors, a full service law firm. She practises primarily in the area of family law. By combining common sense and humour, Norma has shown thousands of people how to successfully survive their separation and re-emerge happy, healthy and emotionally and financially sound. A frequent guest on TV shows, and a much sought-after speaker, Norma lives in Toronto, Ontario with her husband, Ronauld G. Walton.

The

Seven

Steps

to

a

Successful

Separation

# The Seven Steps to a Successful Separation

## COMMON SENSE TIPS

## TO SURVIVING

## THE BREAKDOWN OF

## YOUR RELATIONSHIP

Norma Walton

Perspectives Publishing House

Copyright @ 2000 by Norma Walton

All rights reserved. No part of this publication may be
reproduced or transmitted in any form or by any means,
electronic or mechanical, including photocopying, recording,
or any information storage and retrieval system,
without permission in writing from the publisher.

Published in 2000 by
Perspectives Publishing House
A division of Global Perspectives Inc.
820 Mount Pleasant Road
Toronto, Canada   M4P 2L2.

First printing
July 1999

Canadian Cataloguing in Publication Data

Walton, Norma   1970-
The Seven Steps to a Successful Separation

ISBN # 0-9685685-0-5

1. Legal advice, personal   I. Title

Although the author has attempted to ensure the accuracy
and completeness of the information contained in this book,
we assume no responsibility for errors, inaccuracies, omissions, or any
inconsistency herein. Any slights of people or organizations are
unintentional. Readers should use their own judgment and consult a
lawyer or attorney for specific advice before making any legal decisions.

All the characters in this book are fictitious. Any resemblance to
actual persons, living or dead, is purely coincidental.

Editor:   Ronauld G. Walton
Cover Design:   BTT Communications
Cover Photograph:   Jan Becker
Typesetting:   Jeff Gerstl
Hair and makeup:   Maurice Fiorio

Printed in Canada

# Acknowledgement

First of all, I would like to thank my husband and partner, Ron Walton, for his unfailing love, support and great sense of humour throughout this endeavour and in all other aspects of our lives. He edited the entire manuscript tirelessly and with wisdom.

    Secondly, thanks again to my parents, Myrne and John Rawlings, for their constant encouragement and exhortation. To my parents-in-law Norene and Gordon Walton for their support, company and care. To my sister-in-law, Wendy Preiano, for her tenacity, creativity, dedication, marketing of the book and strawberry-banana smoothies. To my friend, Elvina Verna, for her unfailing generosity, loyalty and great food. To my brother and sister-in-law, David and Tasha Rawlings, for their friendship.

    Third, thanks to everyone at Walton Advocates who helped, encouraged, shouldered work for me, covered for me, and kept me company while writing this book, and specifically to Danka Milutinovic, Olga Dmochowska, Jackie McKinlay, Laura Mackay, Jeff Gerstl, Sheila Kalinovits, Karen Thrasher, Rachel Russell, Leslie Staddon, Sarah Eisner, Mary Ferns, Natasa Milutinovic and Jordan O'Connor. And thanks to John St. James, for his helpful suggestions.

    Finally, to all of my clients, who make my job enjoyable and without whom I would not have learned all of these valuable lessons: thank you.

To Ron

# CONTENTS

## THE SEVEN STEPS TO A SUCCESSFUL SEPARATION
### by Norma Walton, B.A., LL.B.

| | | | |
|---|---|---|---|
| 1. | Separated and Scared | | *1* |
| 2. | Step One: | Know Your Rights | *19* |
| 3. | Step Two: | Seek Help | *45* |
| 4. | Step Three: | Focus on Your Children | *73* |
| 5. | Step Four: | Take Half the Cash | *99* |
| 6. | Step Five: | Consider Mediation | *115* |
| 7. | Step Six: | Make It Enforceable | *131* |
| 8. | Step Seven: | Expand Your Horizons | *141* |
| 9. | Starting Over | | *153* |
| 10. | Appendix A: Resources | | *161* |
| 11. | Appendix B: North American Law Societies & Bar Associations | | *169* |
| 12. | Appendix C: Sample Financial Statement and Budget | | *181* |
| 13. | Appendix D: Information Your Lawyer Will Want to Know | | *187* |

# PREFACE

A "Successful Separation" seems like an oxymoron or misnomer. How can a "successful" relationship break down? Certainly being separated may not at first seem very "successful." Yet there are people who are ruined by separation and others who, through their thoughts, behaviours and actions seem to learn from the experience. They use the crisis of separation to improve as people.

No one ever plans for their marriage or relationship to end in separation. Yet 50% of all American marriages and 38% of all Canadian marriages end in divorce. There are no statistics on common-law and same-sex relationship breakdown but one can assume the numbers would be similar.

Separation and divorce are the most traumatic events that can befall you next to the death of a spouse or a child. Your spouse leaves and you are forced to deal with turbulent emotions and shattered hopes while juggling difficult financial circumstances and your children on your own.

Before separating, however, I recommend that you consider reconciliation counselling if appropriate. If you can save your relationship and it has the potential to be loving and fulfilling, reconciliation counselling is an excellent investment. However both spouses need to attend counselling to change their behaviour and the relationship. All too often, reconciliation counselling is used by one spouse to blame the other for all the relationship's problems.

What are the successful attitudes and behaviours that can be adopted to best survive your separation? After studying this phenomenon over the past decade, I have compiled seven steps which can help you to manage your separation and emerge a better person. As outlined here, I have attempted to keep the steps simple and straightforward. All you require is the desire to learn. These steps will allow you to change your attitudes, behaviours and thoughts to ensure you emerge from the separation intact and healthy, improved emotionally, financially, spiritually and physically.

This book will educate you on basic family law in North America, although each state and province varies somewhat in its specific laws, practices and application. It is critical that you determine your own state or province's specific laws before making any important decisions.
Hopefully you can use the steps relayed here to improve yourself, your life, and that of your children.

I have developed certain practices over the years in my family law practice. First, I try to understand the emotional and psychological pressures and stages which a person experiences upon separation. Second, I try to put myself in your shoes when discussing money, goals, children and your frustrations. I believe the best gift you can give your children during separation is not to involve them, not to put them in the middle, and instead to be focussed on their well-being. I believe it is important to be assertive and stand up for yourself and your rights and entitlements. That being said, you need to choose your battles wisely. Fighting about everything is enervating, expensive and senseless. Finally, I believe in treating people the way I would like to be treated.

This has led to me having wonderful, caring, fun, humourous clients who will I hope enjoy this book and see some of themselves in it. My clients will recognize their success stories in the pages of this book.

Finally, I always tell my clients that the year of separation and divorce will be very difficult - usually the worst year of their life. But things *do* improve with time. Hopefully, this book will speed the healing process and help you have a successful separation.

Norma Walton

# 1

## SEPARATED AND SCARED

I used to love April! A new beginning, I felt. Michael and I would drive up to Horseshoe Valley on Saturdays and hike through the woods, marvelling at the birds starting to sing, he and I cuddling and kissing, laughing and sweating. I would take photographs and he would go for runs.

I had met Michael at Princeton in my third year. He played basketball - a real jock! He always had a lot of male friends around. I was quieter, more artistic, sensitive. I was a loner and amazed by Michael's constant entourage of friends. I admired him from a distance.

Michael and I had met in April. Finals were nearing, and I remember one evening I dragged myself over exhausted to the laundromat on campus. I began one load and was reading my art history textbook while my laundry rotated, when Michael walked over. I would later learn this was typical Michael. Forgetful, bold, confident, charming. Everything I was not.

"I need soap," he stated, interrupting me from my reading.

Looking up into his handsome, inquiring gaze, I began blushing. I must have looked a mess.

Crimson, I handed him my value box of Tide, fumbling with it and looking down. He began his wash and we began talking.

I was not Michael's type. He liked tall, beautiful model types - thin, willowy girls who painted their toenails a different colour every day, always coordinating with their nails - and smiled no matter what Michael said. I instead was clumsy, on the short side and had a pudgy tummy. I wasn't ugly nor was I beautiful. My grandmother called me "handsome," and a prior boyfriend had called me "cute." I called myself "creative" and left it at that.

But something clicked at the Laundromat. It turned out we were both from the East Coast. I had been born in Halifax; he in Boston. Our families had both rented cottages on the South Shore in Nova Scotia every summer when we were young. Becoming more comfortable, I described to him my recent trip to Provincetown and the paintings I had created there. He was surprisingly interested, and we talked until my four loads and his one load of laundry were done.

He walked me back to my apartment. My room-mate and best friend, Sandy, was visiting her parents so I had the apartment to myself. Feeling emboldened by Michael's interest, I invited him in. Walking in he noticed the canvas I had been painting. He immediately took control and did a full tour of the tiny apartment. It was a mess but he didn't seem to notice. I learned later that he never noticed messy.

"Wow! These are incredible." he yelled. "This eagle - the eyes are so real, so powerful and proud." I was flattered he liked my paintings.

We talked for hours in the apartment about all sorts of things: my loving father, recently dead; my over-reaching mother; his doting mother; his dead father. We had a lot in common. I really felt he understood my feeling of abandonment when my father died.

We discussed what we thought of university. I described to him my recent essay on "The Sex Life of Snails" and he described basketball practice. I could imagine his sweaty, half-naked body running around the court.

Then we kissed. And kissed. And kissed some more. Michael was an exquisite kisser. He was the first man I had sex with within six hours of meeting him. He was only my fourth lover. I learned later I was his twenty-fourth. Within two days, we were living together in his cramped apartment and we had been inseparable from that day forward.

Until April 14, 1997, that is.

Michael's words first thing that fateful morning were still ringing in my ears: "This just isn't meeting my needs. I can't handle it. I've met someone else."

How can something so right suddenly not "meet his needs?" I was still reeling as he spoke. Apparently, he had met her at work. She was a new associate there, in training to be a broker's assistant. Her name was Jennifer Somers. She was tall, model-like, stupid. The type of woman Michael used to date before he and I were married. The type of women he had assured me during countless lovemaking sessions that he didn't want. Could never want. He loved me too much. I fulfilled him. I need never worry. My body, with all its pudgy, adorable crevices, was what he loved. He would never leave me. He wouldn't be able to live with himself. He was too honourable to ever do that.

Having always believed him, I was in shock. How hollow his statements now seemed.

Michael and I had always been opposites. But in my mind, it had worked. We were married on October 10, 1984: What a day! Two weeks after our fourth-year convocation. It was on the beach in Hawaii. Over the objections of our mothers we had opted for simple instead of elaborate. They had grudgingly come along and actually enjoyed themselves. The view that day was majestic. I have been painting for years from our honeymoon photographs.

Jennifer had waltzed into what was otherwise a pretty good life and ruined it. She was, of course, younger than me, prettier than me and, obviously, "met Michael's needs" better than I did.

What to do now? Where to turn? My life was shattering around me. Yet I still faithfully took the children to slow-pitch that evening. Kent and Jeff loved baseball. They could name all of the Toronto Blue Jays with corresponding numbers. I never understood their interest, preferring to stay at home and paint than venture out to a sporting event. That had always been Michael's territory. But Michael was off with Jennifer. And the boys had to go to baseball.

"Hi, Marge," I greeted the coach's wife when we arrived at the field. "Samantha, it is so good to see you. It's been a long time since I saw you at a game. Where's Michael?" Good question, I thought silently. How to answer this woman? She had been married for thirty years to Bob. How would she understand that I no longer met Michael's needs. "He's busy today." I replied feebly. How was I going to handle the questions that were sure to come. My mother's would be "What did you do wrong?"

The truth would be out soon enough. I was sure everyone in the park could see the sign over my head: "Sam no longer meets Michael's needs." I felt like such a conspicuous failure. I had read about people going through divorce. I had read about the money spent, the difficulty finding a good lawyer whom you could afford, the emotional trauma and the cost to the kids. I had read about how men were usually better off after divorce, whereas women were worse off. I never thought it would happen to me. How many other women had felt the same and seen that belief shattered, stomped on, and obliterated before their eyes. I wondered.

I had suspected for years that Michael was hiding something from me but I kept telling myself I was crazy. Michael told me all the time that he would never leave. He became offended, his honour bruised, when I raised doubts about his fidelity. I figured he was right. I was just paranoid. Michael told Kent and Jeff when they talked about school chums whose parents were divorcing "You will never have to worry about that." Until April 14, 1997, he forgot to say.

"You'll never have to worry about divorce." I felt set up. I felt betrayed. And yet I still loved him. At least I thought I did. Then again, what was love? What did it really mean?

When Michael and I were in university, we had attended all of the varsity parties, always ending up in a room upstairs having sex at the end of the night. Michael seemed to enjoy the thrill that someone could walk in at any time. I loved sex with Michael so I was usually obliging no matter where he wanted it. We once had sex in the basement of a parking garage, with me giggling and him panting. It was great. Looking back now, that seems another lifetime, another person.

Michael and I moved to Toronto in the mid 1980's. We initially considered New York City and Boston, but the crime rates in both cities were terrible at that time and we wanted to have children. Back then, the exchange rate wasn't so bad, and housing prices in Toronto were reasonable.

Upon graduating with his honours Business Administration Degree from Princeton, Michael was a highly regarded recruit for Finney and Wallace Securities. They paid to move us to Toronto and provided us with four months' accommodation in a hotel while we found a home. I initially worked at an advertising agency, Blue Heron Communications. The job was obtained through a contact at Michael's office. I loved the creative as much as I detested the competitive aspects of my job.

Kent was born on February 1, 1988. Michael and I decided I should stay home with him until he was in school full-time, so my maternity leave turned into full-time homemaking. I loved being at home, loved watching Kent grow up. I was happy to stay home, paint, make Michael's dinner, and raise Kent. My best friend, Sandy, had teased me that I had become a housewife. She was concerned I was making sacrifices for Michael. In fact, I wouldn't have had it any other way. On June 4,

1991, Jeff was born, nixing any thought of my returning to work. I had been home for nine years now.

I remember a day within his first two years at Finney and Wallace Securities when Michael came home in despair that someone else who had started with him had been promoted over him. I told him his time would come. It did and in a big way. Michael was good at company politics, something that I never understood. He had clawed his way up the ladder to be a vice-president. He earned a good salary and an even better bonus in good years. And there had been a number of good years. I earned very little selling paintings from time to time. Nevertheless, I was a great mom, I thought.

I had always seen the marriage as a good partnership. Michael's salary was low at first. I was always there in those early years to encourage Michael and bolster his spirits. But after Kent's birth, Michael's salary and bonus rose significantly, and we managed okay. Now I sold art more as a hobby than a career. It hadn't been a significant portion of our family earnings since Kent was born. Michael always teased me that it was my mad money.

Michael was expansive and loved being the centre of attention, the life of the party. I had always preferred to be in the background, away from the limelight. At first, Michael would insist that I accompany him to company functions, always doing his best to draw me out of my shell and introduce me to women I would like. But over the years, the essential functions I had to attend dwindled and I was quietly relieved. Michael began to like going by himself. I was happy with that. I never figured it would affect our relationship.

As far as I knew, Michael and I had only joint bank accounts. I had a spousal Registered Retirement Savings Plan which he controlled. I knew nothing about our finances. He had always taken care of that. I disliked balancing cheque books, primarily because mine never balanced. Michael, on the other hand, was a financial wizard. He could solve complicated arithmetic problems in his head never putting pen to paper. He loved to talk about statistics, teaching the boys hockey and baseball statistics that I could never understand. I had no idea how on earth I was ever going to survive this separation financially without going bankrupt. What was a spousal Registered Retirement Savings Plan anyway?

The morning Michael left, he packed an overnight bag with his clothes and toiletries and drove off. He said nothing to the children. He didn't kiss me goodbye, nor did he say much. I was in shock. I didn't scream or shout, just sat there numb, disbelieving. Our entire relationship flashed through my mind. Michael had always needed the spotlight. He still played hockey with "the boys" always telling me stories of how he could skate circles around the others. He had been in the hospital room when Kent was born, and I remembered how tender he had been, scared to break him. When Jeff was born Michael claimed he was too busy at work to be there. I now wondered just what sort of work he had been doing.

I was an only child. My dad had died of a heart attack when I was nineteen years old in my second year at Princeton. All I remember about him are smiles, hugs and encouragement. He made me feel so loved, so special - and then he died.

My mom tried to be nice but I found her irritating. She was always wanting to take me shopping. I hate shopping. I find malls so confining. I'd rather be outside taking photographs or in my studio painting. Dad used to understand that, telling me I was a genius with a paintbrush and sitting for hours watching me work, letting me paint him for practice. That smile. That support. Wow, could I use it now!

Dad had run his own business, a Ford dealership in Halifax, Nova Scotia. He was always helping people, often giving away his last loaf of bread and lending cars to people who couldn't afford them. He was fabulous. I needed him. I looked into the sky and said hello to him, told him about Michael and asked for his help. I believed in angels, and Lord knows I needed a guardian angel right now!

Mom became even more over-reaching after Dad died. She had some money from insurance he owned, and she began putting on airs about how important she was. She bought a mink coat - used, although no one but me and the former owner knew that. She would wear that coat in the middle of summer just to show she had the money to buy a mink. Mom loved Michael. Thought he was good for me. "Too good for me, mom. I no longer meet his needs."

That was what she would say too, I feared. Mom and Michael were pals immediately, with him squiring her in her mink around town in his 1980 Mustang with the souped-up wheels. Mom would be devastated by what had happened.

---

I took Kent and Jeff to school on April 15th. They asked where their father was. "Your father had to leave on a business trip last night. It was unexpected. He said to tell you 'he loves you.'" What else do you say to a nine and five year old?

Once their lunches were packed and they were delivered to school, I came home and went back to bed. What to do? What to do? At around noon, I dragged myself out of bed and called Sandy. Sandy was my best friend in the world. She had always been there for me. Michael teased during the marriage that she loved me more than he did. Right about now I agreed with him.

I had known Sandy for twenty-four years which was eleven years longer than I've been married to Michael. We met at Wepabachi Summer Camp in Huntsville, Ontario. We hit it off immediately. Sandy is as tall as I am short and as assertive and aggressive as I am passive.

The first day at camp, we snuck off together, leaving our group and wending our way to the waterfront. I have always loved sitting on the end of a pier, staring into the water. Sandy shared my enjoyment, although she kept skipping rocks off the pier while we sat. She told me about her family. She described her step-brother, step-sisters and her step-mom. Her real mom left the family when Sandy was an infant, and her father, after the divorce, had remarried in less than a year. Her step-mom, Bonnie, was really nice to her. Her dad was much stricter and liked to yell. Sandy and he often fought. All of her siblings were younger than she was, so she'd been forced to develop leadership skills.

Sandy was the unofficial god-mother of my boys, and they called her "Auntie Sandy". She in turn, having no children of her own, doted on them as if they were hers.

At that pier oh so long ago, I had told her about my dad and my mom, and my fears and insecurities. We'd always been comfortable together. Moreover, Sandy had never hurt me. She and I moved to Princeton at the same time and were room-mates. Until I met Michael.

Sandy and Michael had always enjoyed an easy relationship. They were similar in their love of sports and both had been very popular at school. Why they both liked me so much I had never understood.

"Michael has just left." Flat, unemotional. There it was. "He said I no longer met his needs." Another statement. Flat. Sandy was her typical self. She was over by 12:10 p.m. She hugged me while I cried quietly.

Sandy sat next to me while I called my mom. "Mom, Michael has left me." I blurted out rather than saying hello.

"What did you do?" she inquired.

"Nothing, mom. I no longer meet his needs."

"Do you need me to come?" she asked. "I can be on the next bus."

"Thanks, mom, but Sandy is here right now. I may need you later. Thanks." I hung up feeling worse.

"You need a good lawyer." Sandy stated once I had stopped crying.

"Sandy, I don't want a lawyer. I feel like garbage and don't have any money," I protested.

"No matter what you feel like, you need a good lawyer," she insisted. "Let me call Ruth. Her sister just went through divorce. I'll find out whom she used."

DIVORCE. I had avoided thinking about divorce. That country song about D-I-V-O-R-C-E flashed through my head. Michael leaving had been one thing, but my marriage ending in divorce? I had known it wouldn't happen to me. Michael told the kids it would never happen. I had believed him. DIVORCE! My poor boys. Poor me.

Sandy was on the phone. "Nora Conway? 484-8900. Thanks, Ruth."

Nora had a cancellation the next day, and squeezed us in on Ruth's recommendation. Sandy obtained the appointment. She then made dinner for me and the kids. My favourite - shepherd's pie with tiramisu for dessert.

That night, I couldn't sleep. All I kept thinking about was DIVORCE. At 7 am Thursday, I woke the children and readied them for school. My appointment with Nora was at 11 am. I wore my new blue sweater and a white skirt. I hoped I looked appropriate. I had never been to a lawyer's office before. Michael had handled all the legal transactions in the past. I picked Sandy up on the way.

"I am so thankful for your help," I told Sandy. "What would I do without you?"

Best friends and husbands. There were a lot of books about that. Did it ever happen. I turned to Sandy and asked her. She nodded and began telling me about her friend, Ruth's sister. Gretchen had been married for almost 40 years. She had polio as a child and had overcome a lot of disadvantages. She had a great personality. Her husband, George, was a police officer. Sandy related how one day, Gretchen came home early to find George in bed with Gretchen's best friend, Jill in her master bedroom. Her master bedroom, and there was her husband and best friend.

I gasped. I couldn't handle that. "What happened?"

"A lot of screaming ensued, Gretchen fell over and broke her shin and George took her to the hospital. They attended counselling for one year to try to make things work. Then Gretchen caught him talking on the phone with Jill and she ended it."

Gretchen had a lot more confidence and pride than I felt at that moment. "How do you ever heal from something like that?"

Sandy, always confident, replied: "Psychologists say there are a number of psychological stages that people go through after separation: denial, then anger, followed by sadness, loss, acceptance and resolution."

I wondered where I was at? Do I deny that Michael walked out? No. But do I believe our marriage is over? No. Denial. Yeah, maybe. But I don't think you can ever self-diagnose.

"Sandy, what stage am I at?" I asked.

"Denial," she confirmed with a smile. "I'll let you know when you should move to anger," she said, her smile broadening. I smiled too. Sandy could always cheer me up.

Sandy explained: "Some psychologists believe that separation is the most difficult trial anyone can endure in a lifetime. You feel rejected, disillusioned, jealous, violent." Separation was certainly the hardest thing I'd yet encountered, and I thought my mother was my cross to bear!

Nora was late. Her receptionist, Sheila, was nice, and the lobby magazines were current. Sandy and I talked while I flipped through *People*. At 11:15 am, she entered the lobby. She looked younger than I thought she would be, yet she had kind eyes and a firm handshake. Her office was bright, sunlit and comfortable.

"This is a free half-hour consultation," she explained. "I need to take some general information from you, and then you can ask me any questions you wish."

Questions. I hadn't considered questions. I began to panic until I noticed Sandy removing a list from her purse and spreading it on Nora's desk. She looked over and winked at me. I was relieved I could count on Sandy to think for me at a time like this.

Nora asked my name, address, date of birth, employment history. She asked about my children. She then asked how she could help.

"Well," Sandy explained, "Sam's husband walked out on her two days ago. He is having sex with a much younger co-worker. He took his personal belongings and just left."

Nora looked sympathetically at me, then asked more questions. "What is his name? Date of birth? Where does he work? Do you know where he is staying now? What does he earn?" She asked about our assets and debts. Then she began explaining about family law.

# 2

## STEP ONE:
## KNOW YOUR RIGHTS

"When did you marry Michael?" Nora asked.

"October 10, 1984," I replied.

"First, let's discuss marriage," Nora said. "What makes a valid marriage?"

Silence.

"Well, let me put that another way," said Nora. "What kind of marriages are not valid?"

Sandy began: "Well for one thing, gay couples cannot marry in North America. Only people of the opposite sex can marry." This was important to Sandy because she had a gay step-brother.

"In most states and provinces, that's right," said Nora. "You may see the law change in the next 20 years on that subject, but right now same-sex couples cannot marry. What else?"

"Children can't marry," I said.

"Right again," Nora said. In North America, spouses have to be at least 16, 18 or 19 years of age, depending on the state or province. If they are not yet that old, a parent can consent to the marriage or a judge can allow it. Otherwise, they cannot marry. What other factors are needed to marry?"

"You can't be too drunk to understand," jibed Sandy.

"Actually, you're right," was Nora's reply. "Each person must understand what he or she is doing and must understand the consequences of marriage. Each person must marry voluntarily. The term shot-gun wedding refers to a situation where a fellow impregnates a gal and is then forced to marry her because her father is standing at the back of the church with a shot-gun. In North America, that marriage may not be valid because the fellow married under what we call duress."

"That's because he got under the dress!" Sandy joked.

Nora smiled.

"You can't marry your step-brother," said Sandy. Again, this was something relevant to her given her many step-brothers and sisters. "And you can't marry someone if you are already married."

"Exactly," said Nora. "That basically covers who can and cannot marry."

"You need to agree to marry," I said. "But shouldn't you need to agree to separate too? How can Michael just walk out on me without my consent?" I asked, trying not to sound too self-pitying, and at the same time fighting back tears.

"That's a good question," Nora responded. "A couple does not have to agree to separate. One person, like Michael, can decide he wants to end the marriage and he can cause a separation without your consent."

"That doesn't seem fair," I replied. "We went into marriage together. We decided to have children together. Why can Michael just leave?"

"I suppose it is for practical reasons," Nora replied. "If one person is no longer interested in fulfilling his or her marital role and obligations, there is very little a judge can do to make that person stay."

"Michael told me he was going to obtain an immediate divorce. Can he? Don't I have to consent to divorce?"

"Michael may be able to obtain a divorce in time, but very few Judges would give him one immediately. First, he needs to take care of his responsibilities to his children and to you," Nora explained.

I let out a sigh of relief. "At least he should lose all his legal rights to the property and children if he walks out," I stated, hoping it was true.

"No, in most provinces and states, behaviour is irrelevant unless it affects one spouse's ability to parent his or her children." Nora replied. "Samantha, do you know what the grounds for divorce are in North America?" Nora asked.

"Well, I've heard about the uncontested or no-fault divorce. I assume that means if both of you agree?"

"Partially true. A Judge can grant a divorce if there has been a breakdown of the marriage. 'Breakdown of the marriage' generally can mean three things in North America. In your case, you can sue Michael for divorce because he has committed adultery with another woman. That is one ground for breakdown of the marriage. Or you can sue him for divorce on the basis of one year's living separate and apart. In North America, the time you need to live apart varies from a few months to three years. Because the two of you live in Canada, you have to wait one year before you can obtain the divorce on this ground. The third reason for breakdown of marriage is if Michael had treated you with physical or mental cruelty of such a kind as to render continued cohabitation intolerable. Those are the three main grounds for divorce," Nora explained.

"Doesn't leaving someone with two children qualify as mental cruelty?" I queried.

"No, Samantha, mental or physical cruelty has to be such that it renders continued cohabitation impossible - such as physical abuse, forcing one spouse to be treated in a cruel manner, or encouraging the children to hit that spouse. Those sorts of things. Most of the time, spouses will fight a divorce if those sorts of behaviours are alleged."

I was horrified by the thought of divorce.

## Step One: Know Your Rights

DIVORCE! At the same time, I wanted Michael and Jennifer to suffer. "Could I somehow embarrass Michael's new flame?" I asked sheepishly.

"Yes," replied Nora. "You could name her in your divorce petition against Michael."

"Would she need to know I had named her?" I inquired.

"Yes, if you name her, you must provide her with a copy of the petition for divorce." Nora replied.

"What sort of proof do I have to provide the court to obtain a divorce on the grounds of adultery?"

"You need to convince a court on balance of probabilities that Michael is having sexual relations with his co-worker, and that you did not condone his behaviour. If a third party also knows about his adultery, they could testify with you to bolster your case."

"Could the court force Michael to admit he is in fact having sex with another woman?" I queried.

"No, unfortunately the court cannot demand that Michael answer direct questions about the adultery, although he can admit the adultery voluntarily," Nora replied. "If he won't admit it, the judge will have to rely solely on your testimony and any objective evidence, for example from a co-worker of Michael, one of his friends, or a medical practitioner proving Michael gave you a sexually transmitted disease."

"What about the divorce on the basis of one year's separation? When does the year start running?" I asked. "Is it once Michael and I are legally separated?"

"The year generally dates from the time at least one spouse, in this case Michael, has the intention of living separate and apart from you and acts on it," Nora replied. I assumed that him leaving me the morning of April 14 and not coming back probably qualified.

Nora continued. "I've had a number of spouses live 'separate and apart' under the same roof. One of my oldest clients still lives in the same house as his spouse even though they are divorced. Living separate and apart is all about intention to live separate and apart emotionally."

Sandy was intrigued. "How can one of your clients live with his ex-wife in the same house?"

"Well, they are both in their eighties, and they have a duplex that neither wanted to leave or sell. Thus, they've divided the house and each continues to reside in his or her separate section."

"Doesn't this create major problems?" Sandy asked.

"No, they've been together for more than 50 years. People often say hate is the opposite of love. In fact, I believe apathy is the opposite of love.

These two hate each other, and I think continuing to live together gives them purpose and satisfaction. My client, the husband, likes the house cold at night, so he adjusts the thermostat to 15 degrees every night. His wife likes the house at 25 degrees at all times, so she will sneak down in the middle of the night and turn it back up. They seem to take comfort in continuing the fight," Nora explained.

"War of the Roses, Part II," I said.

"Yes, something like that," Nora replied.

"The ground of divorce on the basis of mental cruelty sounds difficult to prove," noted Sandy.

"It is. Physical cruelty is easier to prove because it usually involves physical or sexual assault. Mental cruelty is more subtle. Examples are threatening physical violence towards a spouse or the children, or constantly denigrating and screaming at your spouse in public. 'Being mean' doesn't qualify."

"It sounds like the easiest way to obtain a divorce is to wait out the year of separation," I remarked.

"You're right," said Nora.

"So Michael can't obtain a divorce before a year has passed?" I asked tentatively.

"Yes. Michael's comments about divorcing you quickly are not realistic," Nora assured me. "As the adulterer, Michael cannot sue for divorce on the basis of his adultery. Only you can sue on that basis. As you haven't been cruel to him, he'll need to wait at least one year before obtaining his divorce."

"Are you automatically divorced after one year?" Sandy asked.

"No," Nora replied. " You need to give your spouse proper legal notice that you wish a divorce and then proceed to court to request your divorce from a judge. A divorce must be granted by a judge. It is not automatic."

Knowing that Michael couldn't rush to court and divorce me without providing for me and the kids made me feel a lot better.

"Sam is Catholic, Nora. She'll need an annulment, not a divorce, won't she?" Sandy asked.

"Actually, she will need both a divorce and an annulment."

This sounded expensive!

"The Catholic Church grants annulments at its sole discretion, but that does not affect the *legal* validity of your marriage. Thus, you need a divorce to remarry and you need an annulment to remarry in the Catholic Church. An annulment granted by the Church is different from one granted by the courts."

"Can't you annul a marriage if you are sexually dissatisfied with your spouse?" Sandy inquired. This was new to me. I had never been sexually dissatisfied with Michael - at least until now.

"No, Sandy, sexual dissatisfaction is not enough. There are two types of marriages that can be annulled: a marriage which is *void ab initio* because the spouses did not have the capacity to wed, and a marriage which is *voidable* because an incapacity arises after marriage which entitles one to annul the marriage if he or she wishes."

"Huh?" I was bewildered.

"It's Latin, Samantha." Nora explained. "The first type of annulment - *void ab initio* - means void from the outset. It arises, for example, where a man was already married at the time he purported to marry his wife. If Michael went through a marriage ceremony with Jennifer today, for example. Or if Kent married his girlfriend at school. He's too young to marry so his marriage would be *void ab initio*."

I was beginning to understand.

Nora continued. "The second type of annulment - *voidable* - arises where the husband, for example, is impotent and cannot have children. In that situation, the wife could annul the marriage if she wanted to, although she doesn't need to if she is content to continue in the marriage."

Michael and I had not had that problem. In fact, we'd had great sex throughout the marriage. Passionate, lingering, and satisfying - at least to me.

Why Michael had strayed into the arms of Jennifer I did not understand. I sighed. I was going to miss him in many ways.

"You can deal with all rights and obligations that arise from your marriage without ever obtaining a divorce or an annulment," Nora went on. "A divorce legally ends your marriage and allows one or both of you to remarry. If neither of you want to remarry, or if for some religious or other reasons you are not interested in obtaining a divorce, that's fine. But before you can remarry, you must be divorced."

"So what do I need to do?" I inquired. "If I can't obtain a divorce until one year has passed, can I obtain a legal separation?"

Nora answered. "Actually, the minute Michael left, you and he were separated. A 'legal separation' usually involves a separation agreement, which is a legal contract between a husband and a wife. Both parties must agree to it. No one, not even a judge, can force you and Michael to agree."

I thought back over our marriage. When Michael was being stubborn there was no hope he would agree to anything. I knew that all too well. Michael and I had not fought often, but when we fought he was extremely stubborn and nasty. I made the mistake once of criticizing his mother. I had commented after a trying evening with her that she was very negative and always putting me down. Wow, did he hit the roof! Michael started screaming at me, telling me my mother was a bitch and he hated her. It was unusual behaviour for him, particularly given his good relationship with my mother, which was certainly better than *my* relationship with her. After that, I avoided the subject.

"Can I write my own separation agreement?" I asked.

"You can agree with Michael on all the issues you want incorporated into the separation agreement," Nora responded, "but I recommend you have a family law lawyer draft it for you. These documents are really important and must be done properly."

"But won't it cost us thousands of dollars?" I asked.

"No. In fact, you'll be surprised to know that if you and Michael are able to reach agreement in principle on everything, your separation agreement should cost you less than $1,000 to complete."

"A separation agreement," Nora continued, "must be in writing, signed by you and Michael, and witnessed."

"If we have a separation agreement, do we need to go to court?" I asked.

"No. A separation agreement can settle all issues between you. It has the force of a court order," Nora explained.

"What is the typical process? How do I start the process?" I enquired. I was encouraged about the price, as I believed Michael and I could probably agree on the terms of our separation. I had envisioned wasting thousands of dollars fighting.

"Usually," Nora explained, "we would write a letter to Michael letting him know that you want to negotiate an amicable separation agreement and asking him to have his lawyer contact our offices. Or, if you were able to talk with him, you and he would sit down and discuss the things you want in your Separation Agreement. Once you and he have negotiated a settlement, or once I have negotiated a settlement with his lawyer, it would be incorporated into the agreement for your signatures."

"What if Michael doesn't tell me about all of his financial assets? How do I make sure he's telling the truth?" I asked.

"First of all, we would usually prepare sworn financial statements setting out all of your property and he will set out all of his property. That's the first step in determining whether he is disclosing all of his assets. If you have doubts when you review his financial statement about its veracity, the next step is to request documents backing up his financial information."

"Like bank statements?" I asked.

"Exactly," Nora replied. "Bank statements, investment statements, information and deeds dealing with his ownership in real estate, car ownership documents and valuations, pension valuations, and home appraisals. Anything that backs up the information contained in the financial statement. Once those documents are reviewed, if you still believe he is hiding assets, we can cross-examine him."

"Like Johnnie Cochrane?" Sandy asked with a smile.

"Kind of," Nora replied with a smile, "though generally not in a courtroom in front of a Judge but rather in what we call an examiner's office in front of an official examiner. The examiner will make Michael take an oath to tell the truth and then I'll be able to question him about any parts of his financial statement that you don't believe, as well as about any other financial information you want to know. His answers will be recorded in a transcript which can be entered into evidence in court if needed."

"What if he lies then too?" I asked.

"Well, if the assets that you believe he is hiding are valuable, we could hire a forensic accountant to examine his financial books and records to try to find evidence of those assets. We could also hire a private investigator to determine if he has any assets that he is not disclosing. Finally, we could cross-examine him at trial and leave it up to the judge to determine if he thinks Michael is being truthful. Are you concerned about a specific asset," asked Nora.

"Michael and his sister ran a successful landscaping company while he was in school, and she now runs it yet he continues to be an owner. His sister would do anything for Michael, and I am concerned she will hide company assets or claim it's all hers now."

Nora said reassuringly, "we'll be entitled to review the books and records of the company and cross-examine Michael and his sister if necessary. Try not to worry about it, Samantha. For now, go through all the financial records that remain in the house and copy them for me. That way, if a bank account that you find statements for is not disclosed by Michael, it will give us a sense of whether he is hiding anything."

Even though it was my home too, I was sure I would feel like a criminal rifling through Michael's papers and I would not know what to look for.

Sensing my worries, Sandy piped in, "I'll help you, Sam." Sandy was much more adept at finances than I and her help would be a godsend.

"Once the separation agreement is signed, can it ever be overturned if it turns out Michael was lying?" I inquired.

"Yes, Samantha," Nora assured me. "A separation agreement can generally be set aside if Michael used fraud, misrepresentation, duress or coercion, and also if he failed to disclose to you significant assets or debts existing at the time the agreement was made or if you did not understand the nature or consequences of the agreement."

"Huh?"

"In English, if Michael lies on his financial statement and you find out he lied after the agreement is signed, we can ask a court to overturn the agreement to allow you to share in whatever he was hiding," Nora translated.

"What sorts of things go into a separation agreement?" I inquired.

"Financial arrangements between you and Michael for support of you and the children, the division of your property, custody and access, possession of the home, and any other issue you want to deal with."

I was feeling overwhelmed. "Is there anything I need to do immediately?" I asked.

"Children's issues are usually something you want to deal with immediately. Are you concerned that Michael might come and pick up the children?"

A bolt of terror coursed through me as I contemplated how I would deal with that. After a few deep breaths, I told Nora I didn't think he would.

"Well, even still, we should negotiate some sort of interim agreement to protect you and the children," Nora explained. "We'll discuss children's issues in detail later."

"What is your income, Samantha?" Nora asked.

"Well, I've been home for the past nine years with the boys. I do some painting that I sell to local businesses, which nets me about $10,000 a year. I also still work from time to time as a freelance advertising designer. That probably gives me $8,000 a year. And I have money from my father that generates interest of about $5,000 a year."

"So your total income is about $23,000 per year?" Nora confirmed. "What does Michael earn?"

"I don't know. I expect it is at least $100,000 a year, depending on his bonus, but I'm not sure. I haven't seen his tax return in years."

"You'll probably be entitled to spousal support from Michael." Nora stated.

"But I'm capable of working and I can support myself. Why would I obtain spousal support?" I asked.

"Well," Nora explained, "you have a duty to be as self-sufficient as you can be. But when marriages and common-law relationships break down, the court recognizes your contribution to your marriage and the economic consequences of the marriage to you. Because you have stayed home with the children, freeing Michael to advance his career, he will owe you spousal support because the economic consequences of the marriage have been financially detrimental to you," Nora explained.

"So what you're saying is that I am worse off financially since I stayed home with the children?" I asked.

"Yes. The primary objective of spousal support is to provide compensation for the economic consequences of marriage or cohabitation. Usually this involves compensating women who have assumed the lion's share of household responsibilities and child-care responsibilities to the detriment of their career advancement."

"How do the courts determine the amount of spousal support?" I queried.

"Courts consider all of your and Michael's circumstances, including your combined assets and means, your future assets and means, your capacity to support yourself and Michael's capacity to support you."

"Michael has more assets and more income," I replied.

"He'll need to support you, Samantha," Nora reiterated. "The court also considers your age and physical and mental health, your needs in relation to the standard of living you enjoyed while married, and your plan to become self-sufficient."

"I'm 34 years old. I haven't even thought about becoming self-sufficient. I suppose I need to consider going back to work, don't I?"

"Not immediately, Samantha, but within the next year or so, yes," Nora stated. "The court also considers any obligation Michael may have to support someone else, the desirability of you continuing to stay at home to care for the children, and the contribution you've made to Michael's career."

"So if Michael has to support Jennifer, my support may be reduced?"

"Generally not. You were his first spouse and so he enters his second relationship knowing his obligations to you. Courts will generally not reduce your support because Jennifer also needs support from Michael," explained Nora.

"How long will I be entitled to support?"

"It depends. The current trend is for the court to award a certain amount of spousal support monthly with no time limit, leaving it up to Michael to return the matter to court. Michael would need to prove there has been a material change in circumstances that will decrease or eliminate his spousal support obligation."

"Like what?" I asked.

"Well, if you return to full-time work and

begin earning $100,000 per year, that would certainly qualify as a material change in circumstances," Nora explained.

"I'd be so thrilled to be earning that kind of money, Nora, I would agree that the spousal support end," I stated with a wistful smile.

"If you intend to enter into a separation agreement," Nora continued, "you may need to consider how long you want spousal support from Michael because he is more likely to agree if he knows the support will end at some point in the future. For example, if you intend to be working full-time when Kent and Jeff enter high school, you could schedule support to end on that date."

I had not thought of returning to work. Jeff was five and attending senior kindergarten and my painting did not seem capable of anything other than minimally supporting me. I began to wonder what I would do.

"My brother, Joe, has been living with his common-law partner for the past five years," Sandy stated, "and he's been unemployed for the past six months. If they were to break up, could he claim support from her?"

"Either Joe or his partner could generally claim support from the other," Nora replied.

"He could claim support from her?" Sandy was disbelieving.

"Yes. The courts treat spouses equally

regarding spousal support. If Joe is financially disadvantaged by the breakdown of the relationship and is unable to be self-sufficient, his partner might have to support him."

"But they're not married!" Sandy reiterated.

Nora continued, "in North America, once you have cohabited for between one and five years, depending on the province or state, or have had a child together, either partner can claim support from the other."

"Now back to Samantha's situation. If Michael earns $100,000 per year and you earn $23,000 per year, a court will probably award spousal support between $1000 and $3000 per month."

I was aghast. "Michael will flip. He doesn't bring home enough to pay that!" I exclaimed.

Nora patiently explained, "in most of North America, Michael will be able to deduct whatever amount he pays from his monthly income. This means that he will not have to pay tax on whatever amount he pays you, thus reducing his taxes and increasing his net pay."

"He'll still flip! Is there any way of delaying the payment until he no longer has to pay support for the boys, or some other way of paying it?"

Nora smiled. "Yes, Samantha, you could agree that he could delay it until the children are no longer dependents, although that jeopardizes you because who knows what Michael will be doing in 14 years and who knows whether you will have entered into another relationship."

Another relationship. That was the second brand new thought Nora had prompted. I could not imagine ever trusting another man again. "Why wouldn't I continue to receive spousal support if I entered into a new relationship?" I asked.

"For public policy reasons, courts usually do not like to order spousal support paid from Michael if you have remarried or are cohabiting with another man. So I wouldn't suggest you wait to receive spousal support."

"Okay." I agreed.

"What I would suggest you consider, though, is taking your spousal support as a lump-sum amount from the equity in the home, say, or from Michael's RSPs. That way, Michael would have a one-time payment and would avoid monthly payments, and you would have the benefit of the money in a lump sum now, although you would lose the income stream. We will discuss these options at length. Given your inexperience with finances, though, Sam, you should probably talk with a good accountant or financial advisor about money management."

I figured that with all that money each month, I should be fine and said so.

"Actually, Samantha, financial management

of money is a skill that is learned," Nora replied. "I would recommend you do some reading on the subject. Start with *The Wealthy Barber* by David Chilton and continue with *The Millionaire Next Door* by Danko and Thomas and *Balancing Act* by Joanne Yaccato-Thomas. All those books discuss in detail how you can save money to take care of yourself and your children."

"We're out of time today, Samantha," Nora stated. "I'll prepare and courier a letter to Michael advising him you have retained us and would like to negotiate an amicable separation agreement, and requesting that he contact me. We've covered a lot of ground today, and you'll probably be a little overwhelmed. That's normal. Go home, focus on your children's needs, copy the financial documents in the house for our next appointment, and try not to worry about understanding everything we've discussed. In time, things will come clearer." Nora promised. "Here's your to-do list."

Homework! I smiled. It had been a while since I'd been given homework. First on my list was to attend an appointment with Dr. Morton. Nora had explained that he was a medical doctor and family counselor who helped many of her clients' deal with separation. She had taken the liberty of making an appointment for me the next day. I was apprehensive but grateful. I figured I could use all the help I could get.

I felt better for having met with Nora. On the way home, Sandy and I discussed my to-do list. My next appointment with Nora was on Tuesday. I was pleasantly surprised that Nora had been so understanding. I had been concerned that a lawyer would intimidate and confuse me. Instead I felt I understood my rights and obligations better now and I was encouraged by the spousal support discussion.

I dropped Sandy off at home and picked up Kent and Jeff. "How was school?" I asked.

"Lousy," Kent exclaimed. "Jack McGilvray stole my Nintendo, and the teacher sent me to the principal's office when I decked him."

Dismayed, I looked at Kent. His right eye had a scratch above it, and his eyes were sullen and withdrawn. I stopped the car. "Come here," I said, enveloping him in my arms. I wondered how much longer he would let me hug him. He was nine years old now. Another two or three years and I expected he would be harder to reach. And without Michael around, how was I going to relate to him? Help him through his teenage years. Feeling overwhelmed, I held him tight until he calmed down. Glancing in the rear-view mirror when I resumed driving, I noticed that Jeff had curled up and was sleeping. How do I tell the boys? Everything I had ever heard about divorce said how hard it was on kids.

I pulled by McDonalds on our way home,

which elicited a smile from Kent and a drowsy grin from Jeff. "Three Big Mac meals, please," I requested, "with a lot of extra ketchup, and three root beers." Why not splurge a bit? I might as well enjoy the boys' company before breaking the news about Michael to them.

After dinner, I drove home via the library. The boys and I all loved the library. It had been a favourite haunt when they were not yet in school. I picked up a couple of books on dealing with divorce and breaking the news to children. I checked them out without the boys noticing, and then joined them to choose which books they would take out. Kent settled on a Nintendo book and a book about dinosaurs. Jeff wanted Barney and a book on baseball. We left the library in fairly good humour, considering my last two days.

After the boys were in bed, I read through the book on telling your children about divorce. It warned that divorced children often suffered from depression. It also stated clearly that their reaction was often solely dependent on how you dealt with it. It encouraged reassuring them that the breakup wasn't their fault, and being there to hug and love them. It discussed minimizing the conflict between spouses so the children wouldn't be caught in the middle. It counseled about not making children choose sides. The goal, it seemed, was to arrange custody and access so as to provide love, stability, warmth, and support from extended family or friends and minimize conflict.

I called Sandy. "How am I going to cope?" I began.

"Sam, you'll be fine. You're a survivor. Remember, you survived your father's death; you survived your mother. You'll be okay. You're a great mom, and the boys need you to be as positive as you can be."

I told her what the books had said about children's reactions to divorce. "The books said to be consistent and establish a safe, secure routine for them. How can I do that if I haven't even heard from Michael in more than 48 hours?" I wailed.

"You'll be fine, Sam. The boys love you, they feel safe with you. They're used to you as their main caregiver anyway. They'll weather it. When are you going to tell them?"

"I don't know. I thought the decent thing to do would be to talk with Michael about it. Maybe he and I could tell them together."

"If he's willing, that is probably not a bad idea. Why don't you call him tomorrow to arrange a time to tell the boys?"

"Okay." I yawned.

"Go to sleep, Sam. And stop worrying. You're going to need your strength in the next couple of days."

"Night."

"Night."

I hung up the phone and dozed off to sleep quickly, exhausted from all the thoughts in my head.

The next morning, once the boys were at school, I returned home. I couldn't concentrate enough to paint, and I called to turn down an advertising project I'd been offered because I couldn't think straight. At 11:45 am, the phone rang.

"Hello."

"What the hell is this letter!" Michael screamed. "I tell you I'm leaving and you immediately hire a lawyer? What the hell are you doing? You're going to lose those kids if you keep this shit up. You'll be hearing from my lawyer." He slammed down the phone. So much for talking with the children jointly about the breakup.

Michael's phone call depressed me, and I returned to bed for an hour, alternating between crying and sleeping. At 1 p.m., I arose, ate lunch, and continued reading my books. They described how best to tell children about separation. Well, tonight I'd give it a try. In the meantime, I had my appointment with Dr. Morton.

# 3

## STEP TWO: SEEK HELP

I met with Dr. Morton the next day, being Friday the 17th. Edward Morton. I had always liked the name Edward.

He began as Nora did, asking me a lot of questions about my age, health, the situation, and my children.

"Do you have any specific questions for me, Samantha, or do you want me to fill you in on the different stages of separation and you can ask questions as they arise?" Dr. Morton asked.

"How do I best tell the boys about the separation?" I inquired, wondering if there was a best way.

"Very delicately," he replied. "Ideally you and Michael would sit down with them together. Explain that you are going to separate, meaning Michael will live in another house and they will stay with you. Emphasize over and over again, as many times as you can, that they are not to blame for the separation. Children always believe it is their fault. If they had only behaved better. If they had finished their vegetables at dinner. Children create all sorts of erroneous reasons why they fervently believe they broke up your marriage. You need to reassure them that it's between Michael and you, and has nothing to do with them. Tell them both of you still love them. I suggest you be clear in what you tell them. Don't lay blame. Don't tell them Michael is bad because of the affair. Deal with his new relationship delicately, if at all. On that note, do you know if Michael plans to live with her?"

My composure shattered. Holding back tears, I replied, "I don't know, Doctor. God, I hope not. How would the boys understand that?"

"Best to find out before you sit down with them. Kent and Jeff will want to know," he replied. "The boys will want to know who will leave the house, who will stay, they will want to be reassured that they don't need to change schools or houses immediately. They will want to know if the separation is final. When you tell them, Samantha, try to project calmness and confidence. Let them know you are open for their questions."

I wondered again how I was ever going to accomplish this.

"Other than that question, I don't have anything particular to ask," I said. "Nora Conway booked the appointment for me, and she felt I could use your help."

"I help a lot of Nora's clients," he said. "Anyone going through separation can benefit greatly from counseling. How have you been feeling since Tuesday when Michael left?"

"Really crummy, and confused, and wondering how on earth I am going to manage with the boys."

"Those are normal feelings, Sam. In any separation, there are two parties affected, but they are not affected equally."

Tell me about it, I thought.

"Usually one party has thought about the separation for a long time and has reconciled himself or herself to it. In your case, that's probably Michael. He has accepted that your marriage is over and things aren't working. He has decided that it would be better to separate than to continue to live with you while hiding his adultery. He has commenced a relationship with another woman and in his mind, he has accepted the separation."

"That sounds like Michael," I confirmed. "He seemed so settled and calm about his decision when he left. Meanwhile I felt numb."

"That's not unusual, Sam. You are the spouse to whom separation comes as a shock. Your feelings of numbness are in keeping with the shock. It may be a while before you are able to feel anything about the separation."

That made me feel better. I had initially thought my reaction was weird.

"How did you react when your father died?" Dr. Morton inquired.

"Well, from what I remember, I felt similar to now. I seemed to be in shock and felt abandoned," I replied. "I wondered if I would ever stop crying."

"Separation and death are similar. In both cases, we are losing someone whom we are close to. It's not unusual for our feelings to be the same. You will mourn the relationship the same as you would the death of a loved one. You will feel deep sorrow and grieving. You will reach the deepest sorrow, the death of your hopes and dreams and expectations and memories, during this time. You will doubt you'll ever be whole again. The key during this period is to remember that this too will pass."

I pondered that. I wondered if I would always have an ache in my heart when I thought of Michael. I certainly still ached when I thought of my father, although over the years the good memories came to overshadow the loss.

Dr. Morton went on, "as people we are very good at rationalizing and trying to see the best in a relationship. I've had clients whose spouses have left them cryptic notes - 'This is not working' - and left without ever verbally expressing themselves. I've had other clients who have caught their spouses in adulterous relationships, some even in the master bedroom of their home." I thought of

Ruth's sister, Gretchen.

"I have some clients whose spouses refuse to attend marriage counseling or who become so stressed by raising a child with special needs that they abandon the relationship."

Thankfully, except for Kent's hyperactivity, neither of our children had special needs.

"I have some spouses who lived together for 40 years before one day deciding they had never gotten along and then separating."

The hurt was hard enough after fourteen years of living together. I couldn't fathom forty.

"I have some spouses who discuss and agree upon the separation."

That would have been nice, I thought.

"However it comes about, there's a moment in time when you'll remember realizing that your spouse was no longer committed to the relationship. That's a moment of shock and despair. Some of my clients have considered suicide; others have considered fleeing the city or province or country."

I had not thought of suicide. I couldn't leave the boys. But fleeing home to Halifax had crossed my mind.

Dr. Morton continued. "Shock means that you do not understand the full implications of what is happening. You are numbed and bowled over. You feel awful; sick in the pit of your stomach without quite understanding why."

I had thought I was coming down with the flu. "Dr. Morton, does the sick feeling ever go away?" I asked.

"Yes, Sam, it does. But it takes time. Time is a great healer. In time, everything will be all right again," Dr. Morton reassured. "After shock comes denial. This can't be happening to me. We were soul mates. I was the ideal wife. He, the best husband. You tell yourself that your spouse must be confused and just not thinking properly. He will come to his senses. You will sometimes contact marriage counselors at this point to discuss fees and availability and to set up an appointment."

"My best friend, Sandy, feels I'm in denial already," I said.

"Denial means not accepting that Michael is not coming back. It means not believing this is happening to you," Dr. Morton explained. "Have you been wondering, 'How could Michael do this? He can't mean it. It will all blow over. This is unreal,'" asked Dr. Morton.

"Well, I keep considering Michael's many comments that the boys and I would never go through divorce, and never needed to worry about it. I wonder if it was all talk," I said.

"During the period of denial, you may lose a lot of weight or suffer from insomnia. You will feel your world is surreal and won't be able to comprehend that Michael is not returning."

Losing weight would be great, I thought. Then Michael might come back. Wait a minute, wasn't that what Dr. Morton had just said people in denial think about. I smiled ruefully, and waited for Dr. Morton to continue.

"After denial comes anger. This is the stage where you fantasize about ripping out all the pages in your spouse's prized library or actually do; where you plot your spouse's death in gory detail and maybe even buy *Soldier of Fortune* to find out how much it would cost. Sometimes this is when you take things out on your children or your parents or your friends because you cannot vent your frustration at your spouse."

That would be a relief, I thought. To just feel furious with Michael rather than sick and numb. Bloody angry instead of nauseous. Sounds like a good trade.

Dr. Morton continued, "you think to yourself, 'you can't do this to me.' You feel like a victim and blame your spouse as the instigator of the separation."

"Michael was the instigator, Dr. Morton," I said. "He broke all of his promises."

"True, Samantha. And over time you will come to accept the separation." Dr. Morton replied. "Can I get you a coffee? I am giving you a lot of information and you must be suffering from information overload."

I smiled. "That would be great."

Dr. Morton returned with coffee. It tasted wonderful and I let out a deep breath, contemplating the information he was sharing.

He continued, "after anger often comes bargaining. You think 'I'll do anything you say, just come back.' You make desperate attempts to rescue the relationship. You are terrified of life without the relationship."

I was already terrified about life without Michael. Was Dr. Morton telling me this would get worse? I wondered.

"After bargaining comes depression. This is another period of intense feelings. You'll feel blue, exhausted. You may find it hard to go to work each day. You may be listless and unable to be revived by the company of friends or by activities you usually enjoy. Your emotions turn off. You can't motivate yourself to do anything to help yourself. You may be in a funk for a long time, and it's important that you seek counseling and assistance in going through the emotions of your divorce."

Oh great, I thought, and complained, "Dr. Morton, this process sounds awful."

"It is awful, Samantha, and it's necessary if you are ever going to learn from this relationship, accept yourself, be a good mom to your children, and free yourself to enter a new relationship if desired."

A new relationship. What a joke. I was never letting anyone else get close enough to hurt me.

Dr. Morton continued, "a number of my clients ask if seeking counseling during a divorce will hurt their chances in court."

I had wondered that. Michael had always been opposed to counselors, psychologists, psychiatrists, and the like. He always felt that only weak people sought help.

Dr. Morton explained: "if anything, it will help. Judges expect you to be in emotional turmoil after the breakdown of a relationship. In fact, seeking counseling can be turned to your advantage by a good lawyer to show that you are dealing with the breakdown of the relationship with a professional and that your children are also attending counseling to deal with the breakdown of the marriage. This shows you understand there are emotional and mental aspects to divorce that have a fundamental effect on both you and your family."

I felt a little better. I really liked Dr. Morton.

"Depression will eventually lead to acceptance. Acceptance means realizing the relationship is over. Realizing that there is nothing you can do to change that fact. And being satisfied you've done everything you could."

"That seems a long way off, Dr. Morton," I said. "How long will the process take?"

"Everyone is different, although you will usually need at least one year to progress through the different emotional stages. Acceptance may mean dating again or it may mean never dating again. It generally means being civil to your spouse. It probably means you are now in a position to seriously begin discussing settlement of the issues between your spouse and yourself."

I thought a year was a long time to wait to complete the emotional grieving process. "How can I speed up the process?" I asked.

Dr. Morton smiled. "Many people have asked me that. First of all, attending counseling will speed the process. Reading books about separation and divorce will help as will staying busy and focussed on the children and their best interests."

"Can you guarantee that some day I'll feel okay about the separation?" I asked.

"Once you've accepted that your relationship with Michael is really over, the healing process can begin," Dr. Morton reassured. "After acceptance, you may spend a lot of time wondering about things. You may at first blame yourself entirely for the breakup. Or you may blame Michael entirely. Neither of these feelings is probably accurate."

"I have no difficulty blaming Michael entirely right now, Doctor." I laughed; he laughed with me.

"You may be surprised to know, Samantha, that even though Michael was the instigator, he may feel regret and panic over the separation, wondering what he has done," Dr. Morton explained.

"That would be good, Doctor. It might make him think twice about separating from me and the children."

"Actually, Samantha, you may also be surprised by *your* feelings. The separation may provide you with opportunities in your life that weren't possible while you were in the relationship. You may find that you change some of your habits, your mindset and your activities."

"A period of personal growth, Doctor? What a price to pay for personal growth!" I felt sorry for myself.

"Samantha, personal growth is magnificent. Don't discount it. Growing as a person, becoming better, is the most fulfilling thing we can do in life. Your ultimate goal is to develop or regain your sense of self," Dr. Morton explained.

I asked if couples having sexual relations with each other after separation was normal, as I'd heard it happened frequently.

"During the separation process, you and Michael may briefly reconcile or have a weekend fling. One more kick at the can. It's important to realize that once you have separated, the odds are that you are not going to reconcile with your spouse. You may need to have sexual relations one more time, or dinner one more time, or something one more time, to fully realize that the relationship is over. After this, it is often crystal clear that you have recovered from the separation."

"So you encourage me to lure Michael into bed some weekend?" I said half teasingly and half seriously.

"No, Samantha. But don't feel bad about yourself if it happens. It's not unusual. The difficulty with separation is timing. Right now, if Michael came back, you would probably welcome him with open arms. Yet in six months you may feel a lot differently. And in a year you may feel differently again. Just don't beat yourself up over it if a sexual encounter happens."

I wondered how I would feel having sex with Michael now.

"At some point, you will no longer be emotionally involved with Michael. I've had patients who related seeing their spouse at a joint function for the children. You'll know that you have come to terms with the relationship when you've dealt with the blame, resentment and self-pity and accepted that the relationship has ended. When you're able to see Michael without feeling anything other than a vague sense that he is the father of your children and a former spouse."

"I can't imagine feeling nothing towards Michael," I said. "We've been together so long."

"Everyone is different. The goal is to develop objectivity about the relationship. To view it as completed. Then you can move forward." Dr. Morton clarified.

"Dr. Morton, is it normal to still dream about Michael?" I asked. Thursday evening I had dreamed Michael was in trouble and I hadn't been able to help him.

"It's not uncommon to have vivid dreams about harming your spouse or ill coming to your spouse during the emotional process of separation. It's also not unusual to be incapable of listening to the radio without crying. All of this will pass. If it doesn't, you need the assistance of someone like a psychologist or psychiatrist to help you bring closure to the relationship."

I had turned the car radio off on my way to Dr. Morton's office because I kept weeping when I would hear a familiar song about love and loss. I was amazed that other people felt the same way.

"Relationships by their nature are intense, Samantha. Separation always involves rejection on some level, accompanied with disillusionment and probably jealousy. You shouldn't expect these intense feelings to disappear quickly."

"I hate Jennifer," I confirmed. "And I have never met her."

"That's normal. Don't worry about it. In time, once you have accepted the breakdown of the marriage, your feelings of jealousy will diminish. At this point it's easier to fashion a settlement to meet everyone's needs. You are more reasonable once you accept that your marriage is over and nothing you can do will change that fact. You are a better parent and friend once you reach this point."

"I'm looking forward to completing the stages." I told Dr. Morton.

"It may take very little time to progress through these emotional stages, and you may miss some, but a lot of my clients take a few years to come to accept the breakdown of the relationship. That's okay. Everyone goes at his or her own pace. The important thing is to seek professional assistance if you feel it would help and to obtain professional assistance for your children."

"Dr. Morton, what do you think usually causes separation and divorce? You have counseled a lot of people. What is the reason relationships and marriages break down?"

"There are all sorts of reasons. Some couples blame money management or mismanagement for the separation. Others blame sexual problems or extramarital affairs. Where there is violence, marriages often break down. A spouse with an alcohol or drug addiction will ruin a relationship. Finally, lack of communication will cause a relationship to unravel."

"But isn't there one thing that if avoided will ensure your relationship stays good?" I asked. I was wondering if I could ever picture myself in a relationship again, and pondering what the secret ingredient to a good relationship was.

"I don't know, Samantha. A lot of books have been written trying to define what differentiates a relationship that will last from one that won't. Some experts say it is open communication. Others say it is wanting what is best for your partner. Others say it is common values. I don't have any magic formula. What I *do* know is that you have to start with yourself. You have to learn to like yourself, to be comfortable alone, before you will ever have a successful, happy, long-term relationship. We cannot love another person fully and completely and unconditionally if we don't first love ourselves."

I pondered Dr. Morton's comments for a minute. Did I love myself? I loved Jeff. I loved Kent. I probably loved Sandy. I thought I had loved Michael. I wasn't sure if I loved my mother - I certainly didn't like her much. But myself, loving myself. That was a concept I would have to consider. "So you're saying only I can make myself happy?" I recapped.

"Exactly. No one but you can make yourself happy." Dr. Morton smiled. He was an interesting-looking man. He had extremely kind eyes - blue like sapphires. His wrinkles crinkled when he smiled. He had a mustache - a common characteristic of men who are starting to bald. His hair was obviously thinning, and I expected that the mustache had arrived around the time he first noticed he was losing his hair. He was tall and stocky. Probably 6'2" and weighing 220. I felt comfortable with him. I thought it was probably good to feel comfortable with your divorce counselor. I smiled back at him.

"Your separation can be turned into a positive experience, Samantha, once you deal with the inevitable hurt and trauma it has caused. Your profound pain and disappointment need to subside before you can turn the experience of separation into a life-changing, positive catalyst for self-improvement."

"Other than counseling with you, Dr. Morton, what other activities can I be doing to help myself deal with the separation?"

"Great question, Samantha. First of all, you should go to the library or a bookstore and purchase or borrow a couple of books about separation and divorce. There are great books about reconciliation, self-help, kids and divorce, and new relationships. Reading them can help you realize that you are not alone and that there are common feelings that every separated person experiences."

"Are there books that Kent and Jeff might find helpful as well?" I asked.

"Definitely. Given the frequency of divorce in North America, there are a lot of books to help deal with it, for both children and adults. The second thing you can do is what you are doing. Attending counseling helps you deal with all the tough feelings, emotions and decisions that arise upon separation. If Kent and Jeff seem to be taking the separation hard, they could also benefit from counseling."

"Could they see you?"

"No, Samantha, ideally they will see a child psychologist or social worker who deals with children. Often times Michael's health plan will cover the cost of these professionals when they counsel you or the children. If the boys begin experiencing mental-health problems, like severe depression, for example, they should immediately see a child psychiatrist."

I hoped that neither of the boys would need that much help. I was a little worried about Jeff, my sensitive angel. He did seem a bit despondent and depressed. I vowed to monitor his behaviour to keep him from harm. I would send him to a psychiatrist if his depression continued.

"My best friend, Sandy, has been reading about psychotherapy." I said. "Would I benefit from it?"

"Maybe, maybe not. Psychotherapy is a long process that digs back into your childhood and relates it to the present day to determine the cause of your behaviours and feelings. It's up to you if you want to try psychotherapy. What you and I are engaged in is counseling. Separation counseling. You seem to be doing fine with it. If you feel you need to connect with your past in a more intense way, then psychotherapy may be a good idea."

I confided, "Sandy has been a great support to me, Doctor. She has been my best friend forever, and she's forced me to care for my own feelings and the boys' feelings while still having fun with me. She's one of the only people right now in my life who still makes me laugh."

"Best friends are great sources of strength during separation. Family can be helpful as well. The old expression 'blood is thicker than water' is often on display upon separation. How have your family helped?" Dr. Morton enquired.

"My mom has offered to help with the children while I attend appointments with Nora and with you. That has helped, although I'm not sure her influence in their lives is always positive. She loved Michael, you see, and she thinks I did something wrong, so he left. She keeps telling me to try to win him back."

"In these situations, families can be helpful and destructive at the same time," Dr. Morton reassured me. "Recognize them for what they are, and turn to them for help knowing they are not perfect and will probably irritate you somewhat while doing their best to help."

I questioned him whether he'd heard of "Parents without Partners" or any similar groups.

"Yes. Any groups where separated and divorced people come together will be helpful to you. Just recognize that a lot of what you hear in such a group has a certain bias and you should always make decisions in your and your children's best interests, not in accordance with any specific group's mission statement or biases. Nonetheless, groups like that can be a great support to both you and your children."

"That completes our first session, Samantha." Dr. Morton stated. "I'll see you next Wednesday at 11 am - is that convenient for you?"

"Yes, Dr. Morton. That'll be fine." I left feeling somehow uplifted. On my way home, I stopped at the library again and picked up more books about separation. That afternoon, I read about the number of professionals who could help me and the boys.

The books explained that psychiatrists and child psychiatrists are doctors who have received extensive training in the mental and emotional make-up of people. They can be extremely helpful in assisting with separation. As doctors they can prescribe drugs. Child psychiatrists have a particular skill in dealing with children who go through separation and divorce.

Psychologists and child psychologists, as opposed to psychiatrists, generally have their master's or their Ph.D. degree in psychology and are able to counsel people in dealing with the grief, pain and unhappiness caused by separation.

Social workers, counselors, a family doctor, and other professionals can also assist in dealing with the pain of separation.

After some reading, I realized I had a lot to learn about dealing with separation. I looked through the newspaper and saw a seminar advertised at a place called *New Directions* the next evening. I decided I would attend. Sandy agreed to care for the boys.

Dr. Morton had counseled me to break the news to Kent and Jeff calmly. The books counseled that it would be best if both parents were there, but if that couldn't be arranged, I should explain the situation calmly and without a lot of emotion, and explain clearly that Michael would not be returning to the home. I should tell them when they would see Michael, and what changes they could expect. I should emphasize that separation is between mom and dad and has nothing to do with them, and that their mom and dad deeply love them.

That evening, I asked both boys to come sit

with me on the couch. "I have something I need to talk with you about," I began falteringly. "Dad and I have decided to separate." The shock was evident on their little faces. "It has nothing to do with you, and we both love you more than anything else in the world. It has to do with us. Dad is not happy anymore in the marriage and has decided to leave me. He's not leaving you, and he'll continue to see you a lot. He'll spend weekends with you and will still attend your ball games. It's just that he will no longer be living with us." I surveyed the boys to see the reactions.

"Mommy, it's because I made him mad on Monday," cried Jeff. "I should have never yelled at him and made him purse his lips. Once I tell him I'm sorry, he'll come back, mommy."

"Don't be a baby," said Kent. "I have friends at school whose parents are divorced. Their dad picks them up on Fridays and he's a nice guy."

"Daddy loves both of you very much. Dad and I aren't happy together, but dad will always love you," I explained.

"Can I call him, mom?" Kent asked.

"Sure, sweetie, you can call him. His work number is next to the telephone."

Kent moved to the phone while I held Jeff, who continued to cry in my arms.

"Hi, dad. It's Kent. Mom just told us we're getting divorced. Are you there? Hello. Mom, it's the answering machine." Kent looked crestfallen.

"It's okay, sweetie. Just leave him a message to call you when he gets the message." What to do now? There were still a few hours before bedtime. I didn't want this weighing on their minds for all that time. A distraction? "Let's go rent a movie, okay?" I suggested.

"Okay," both of my little troopers responded. We rented *Mulan* and both boys cried themselves to sleep. I followed suit a few hours later. I hated being a single parent. I had never planned this. How could Michael just leave his family? We were good to him. We had weathered a lot together. I felt so depressed and disheartened and was just drifting into sleep when the phone rang. Not again. I can't handle two nasty phone calls in a day. I finally picked it up after the sixth ring. It was Sandy.

"Sandy, I'm so glad it's you. Michael called earlier screaming, and I broke the news to the boys tonight. It's been an awful day."

"Sam, I'm sorry but you did the right thing. Michael will calm down and things will be okay. I just thought I'd call to see how it went."

"Lousy, Sandy. I'll fill you in tomorrow. Night."

"Night."

Kent brought me the phone at 7:00 the next morning. 7 a.m. on a Saturday! "Daddy wants to talk with you," he said. He seemed okay.

"Michael?"

"Sam. What are you doing telling the boys without me there?"

"You screamed at me yesterday, Michael, and they were wondering where you were. I went to the library, took out a few books on telling your kids that your husband is screwing a younger woman, and just let them have it." I sniped.

"Sam, that's not like you. I just spoke with Kent for 20 minutes. I'm going to see him tonight at his softball game. He seems okay. How did Jeff take it?" Michael sounded relieved that he didn't have to tell the boys. What a bastard.

"Michael, where are you? What number can the boys reach you at? Where are you staying?" I hoped he wasn't about to say Jennifer's place.

"I'm at Bob's place, Sam." Bob was Michael's buddy from Princeton. "I've been looking for an apartment without much success, although apparently my realtor called me yesterday with a lead on a place. Bob's number is 787-0221. I've given it to Kent."

"We need to talk. Can you come over this afternoon?" I pleaded.

"Yes, if you like I'll come over before the ball game."

"Okay. See you then." After I hung up the phone, I heard scurrying outside my door and realized Kent had been listening. I tried to recap my conversation to determine if he had heard anything he shouldn't have. Other than the "screwing" comment, everything else had been okay. The poor kid.

I showered and put on Michael's favourite perfume. I pulled on my sexy underwear, the ones I hadn't worn in years. My shorts were tight, and my t-shirt showed my cleavage. What was I doing? This man had walked out on me and the boys. Why did I want to excite him? In disgust, I ripped off those clothes and threw on my regular stuff to drive the boys to their friends' home. They were spending the afternoon there.

I tried to paint without success. I finished reading the books about separation and divorce. A little dry, but a help. I pondered what Nora had told me.

At 3 p.m. the phone rang. "Sam? Is it okay if I come right now?"

"Sure, Michael."

I hung up the phone, raced upstairs, put on the clothes I was wearing this morning, including the underwear. I brushed by teeth and sprayed on more perfume.

I heard the key in the lock. Michael paused on the threshold, then came inside. "How are the boys?" He asked, after surveying my outfit.

"Fine," I replied. Michael put his hands on

his hips and looked around the room. Then his eyes returned to mine.

"Sam, I'm sorry." In two steps, he was embracing me. "I never meant to hurt you or the kids. I'm unhappy at work, at home, with everything. It's just not fair to subject you and the kids to my misery." He let me go and led me to the couch.

"Jennifer and I are having fun. She's new, she's different. She makes me feel young again."

I felt sick. How could he talk about another woman like that when we had so many years together? And in our house of all places! How could he just throw it all away? I sat numbly while he talked.

"I saw a lawyer yesterday," he advised. "He said we can do everything amicably by agreement. That's what I'd like. I was thinking maybe the boys would want to stay with me for a while, maybe one week of every two." He said this with hesitation.

My mouth fell open. "Not a chance, Michael. You've messed up my life and the boys' lives enough." The anger returned. I looked down at my outfit in disgust. What had I wanted, him to have sex with me again? So we could recapture the magic? What an idiot I must be. "Get out. I will decide what's right for the boys, and when I decide they should see you, I'll let you know." I stormed over and flung open the door.

Michael shook his head, muttered under his breath, and left. I sat on the sofa once he'd gone and wondered whether he had ever loved me? How can someone who loves you ever leave you? Do feelings just change over time, or did they never love you? I felt forlorn and miserable.

I changed into my regular clothes, throwing the tight outfit in the garbage, and went to pick up the boys. I vowed I would not make a fool of myself in front of Michael ever again. Let him have Jennifer. I hoped they both were hit by a truck.

The Saturday evening session at *New Directions* was called "Surviving your divorce" and the seminar leader was named Michael. Despite his name, I still attended. There were fifteen other women in attendance. He began:

"I always recommend you talk with friends who have been divorced and ask them whom they used, or ask your lawyer, who should have a list of reliable professionals who can help you through the pain of divorce."

He discussed a lot of things Nora had already covered, and also discussed trying to maintain a positive attitude.

The seminar content was interesting and the other women were comforting. The seminar leader ended telling us to have hope. Have hope! Things do improve. Keep your spirits up as best as you can. Keep busy. Focus on your children. And pray for the year to pass!

I felt better after the seminar was over. I realized how important it was to seek help from others when going through separation.

The rest of the weekend passed uneventfully. I began painting again. Michael and I had been to Alaska the year before and I had taken some great pictures of the natural beauty. I worked in oils and completed a striking picture of a polar bear. His eyes were sharp and beautiful. He looked angry. No wonder. The painter was angry.

# 4

## STEP THREE:
## FOCUS ON YOUR CHILDREN

At my next appointment with Nora on Tuesday, April 21$^{st}$, children's issues were on the agenda.

I began by asking, "don't I automatically obtain custody because I am the mother?"

Nora replied, "that's a common misconception, Sam. In North America, both parents are equally entitled to custody and there is no presumption that the mother is a better caregiver. That being said, the fact that Michael left you and the children in the home strengthens your claim for custody. It implies he is consenting to you being their principal caregiver."

"He has threatened me in the past when we fought that he would take the children away from me, and he has called me an unfit mother," I said anxiously. "I once got drunk after a fight of ours and he promised to make sure I lost the children because of my drunkenness."

"Courts usually don't care about things like that," Nora reassured me. "They consider your ability to provide for the children's needs, and their primary objective is to place the children with the person who can best meet those needs."

I felt better. I had been worrying about that drunken evening for no reason. Whew!

Nora continued: "courts look out for the 'best interests' of the children. 'Best interests' means the court considers all the needs and circumstances of the child including the love and emotional ties between the child and you, Michael, and any grandparents that care for the child."

"I've always been the principal caregiver of both boys. They're close to Michael and somewhat close to their grandmothers," I explained.

"Good. A court will consider your principal-caregiver role as most important. Courts also consider the views and preferences of the child where the child is able to express such views," Nora continued.

"I think both boys want to stay with me right now," I said.

"Again, good. Courts consider the length of time the child has lived in a stable home environment, the ability and willingness of each parent to provide the child with guidance, education, the necessaries of life, and any special needs of the child."

"The boys have always lived with me and Michael. I don't believe Michael is willing to care for them full-time and I've always provided for their needs," I said.

"Good, Sam. The court will also consider

any plans proposed for the care and upbringing of the child, and the permanence and stability of the family unit."

"Proposed plans, huh? I've been considering returning to full-time work. Will the court give Michael custody if I go back to work full-time?" I asked.

"No, Sam," Nora reassured. "It sounds to me, based on the above criteria, that you will obtain sole custody of the children if you want it."

"Kent takes Ritalin and suffers from Attention Deficit Disorder. Will that be relevant to the court?"

"Yes," Nora replied, "insofar as your ability to meet his special needs is concerned."

"Michael's mom has cared for them from time to time when we have taken vacation. Will a court consider awarding custody to her?"

"No," Nora reassured. "Courts look first to the principal caregivers of the children. It seems to me from what you've said that you were the primary caregiver of the boys since birth and that Michael worked during the day and often into the evening. Typically, courts like to see whatever arrangement was in place before separation continue after separation. They like to disrupt the children as little as possible. Thus, I expect a court will have no difficulty awarding you custody of the children."

"I've heard a lot about joint custody. One of my neighbours - a nice guy - has his kid's one week of every two. Would a court make Michael and I do that?"

"Probably not, Sam," Nora advised me. "Let's start by defining sole custody as opposed to joint custody. Sole custody means that one parent can make decisions for the children without the consent of the other parent. For example, if you had sole custody, you could decide where the children attend school, whether they attend religious services, who their doctor will be, what sorts of programs they will attend after school and on weekends, and other such matters without obtaining Michael's agreement."

"So I wouldn't need Michael's permission?"

"No. If you were the sole custodial parent, it would be your decision alone. Joint custody, on the other hand, requires a lot of cooperation between you and Michael. It means that all those decisions would need to be discussed and agreed upon between you."

"If we can't even agree on whether our marriage should continue, how could we agree regarding the children?" I asked, confused.

"A lot of my clients share joint custody even though they no longer live together. Often the best arrangement for children, if possible, is for both parents to continue to play a very active role in their lives. Joint custody arrangements that work offer the best possible situation for children. My joint custodial parents are able to put aside their personal differences and cooperate in the best interests of the children."

"But I wouldn't want the children, under any circumstances, shuttling back and forth between my residence and Michael's residence every week," I insisted. "As I mentioned, one of my neighbours, Rick, has his two daughters one week of every two. Michael suggested that on the weekend, and I am deathly opposed. I believe the boys need their own room and own home, not two of them."

Nora stated, "joint custody does not mean joint sharing of time. Joint custody means joint decision making as we discussed. Some joint custody arrangements look identical to sole custody arrangements. It has nothing to do with physically sharing time with the children, and everything to do with decision making."

"Oh." I was quite relieved.

"Equal sharing of time works for very few couples. I've had nine couples over the years for whom it worked very well. It requires a commitment by both parents generally to live within walking distance of each other so the children can attend the same school and walk home from school to either parent's home. It also requires constant communication between the parents. Usually the children carry a notebook in which everything that the other parent needs to know is written. Three of my couples have split the week, so that the children spend part of the week with their father and part with their mother. The other three have done one week with mom, one week with dad. As I said, it requires a lot of cooperation and commitment, and is not the norm."

"Will a judge order me to have joint custody with Michael?"

"Typically not, because what a judge would be doing is ordering you and Michael to get along. If you're both in front of the judge so he or she can determine custody, it's a safe bet that you're not able to get along and communicate concerning your children. I've seen situations where joint custody was awarded because the father could show a history of joint decision making after separation and before the court action. Otherwise, Judges will usually make a sole custody order."

"If judges usually won't order equal time sharing, is there a typical custody and access regime?" I inquired.

"Yes, Sam. If a custody and access dispute goes to court, judges will typically award sole custody to one parent and access to the other. The sole custodial parent will usually have the children during the week and the access parent will usually have them alternate weekends and on one or two

## Step Three: Focus on Your Children 79

evenings per week. Often, the Judge will also order sharing of holiday times, including summer, Thanksgiving, December holidays, March break, and any other holidays affecting the children."

"What rights will Michael have as an access parent?"

"He'll be entitled to visit and be visited by the children. He'll also be able to make enquiries and be given information concerning their health, education and welfare."

"Michael's mom lives in Boston. Worst case scenario, what if he picked the children up one Friday night and didn't return with them?"

"Courts and police would do whatever they could to return the children to you. Because Michael and you live in Toronto now, the Toronto court has jurisdiction to make decisions about your children. If Michael were to go to a Boston court for a custody order, that court would probably send him back to Toronto, because Toronto was the children's residence at the time of separation."

"I had a girlfriend in the early eighties who took her two girls, hopped on a plane to England where her family was, and never returned," I said. I had remembered this after Nora asked me in our first session if I was concerned about Michael taking off with the boys.

Nora advised, "if that happened today, the father could probably obtain an Order in Ontario for the girls' immediate return, and then could have the police in England return the children to Ontario. Judges take children's residence very seriously, and they do not tolerate a parent abducting their children. In fact, there have been criminal cases where a parent was charged with abduction and sent to jail."

"Wow," I exclaimed. "The law seems to have changed since my friend did that."

"Yes," Nora explained. "Now let's talk about Michael's threats because you became drunk. Past conduct is not a factor that our courts consider unless it's relevant to your ability to care for the children. So, the fact you became drunk after a fight with Michael does not affect your ability to care for your children and would be irrelevant."

"What sort of conduct would be relevant?" I asked, relieved.

"What would be relevant are physical or sexual abuse of your children, leaving your children unattended while you were out drinking, drug use in front of your children, sexual acts in their presence, and any other behaviour that puts them at risk."

"So I won't lose my children because I became drunk that night?" I repeated.

"No, Sam, you won't."

"What if I were to die, Nora," I asked. "Michael, I assume, would obtain custody of the children."

"Not necessarily. If you had prepared a will where you appointed someone else to have custody, such as your mom or Sandy, for example, a court would strongly consider that appointment when determining who should have custody of your boys."

"Not my mother!" I exclaimed. "I expect Michael would probably be the best person to care for them, being their father. He's actually not a bad father," I offered, "it's the husband part he isn't great at." Nora smiled. I was beginning to like this woman. "How do I obtain custody of Kent and Jeff?"

"There are a few ways," Nora explained. "You can obtain custody by agreement or by court order."

"Is it important to act quickly?" I asked.

"Sometimes, yes. For example, if you thought Michael would abduct them, or if you thought Michael would keep the children and not return them to you, you should act quickly. Do you believe Michael will object to you having custody of the boys."

"I expect he will want joint custody," I said.

"But he won't object to you being their principal caregiver?"

"Probably not."

"Then we can try to negotiate an agreement

or we can bring a motion for interim custody."

"Interim custody?" I queried.

"That means temporary custody until a final order or agreement is made. Don't let the 'temporary' fool you, though. Once you have interim custody, it will be extremely difficult for Michael to obtain sole or joint custody unless you want him to. As long as the children are doing well with you, there would be no reason for a judge to change custody."

"But custody can be changed?" I asked. "I have a friend who had custody of her boys until the oldest turned 14 years of age, then both boys went to live with their father. I think the oldest is now back with her."

"That's not unusual," Nora stated. "No custody order is ever final. As children age and are able to express their wishes, custody often changes. I've seen a lot of 14-year-old boys move to their father's residence. Sometimes it works, other times if doesn't. I've also seen a lot of 15-year-old girls move to their dad's. Again, sometimes it works, sometimes not. So yes, Sam, custody can always be changed. That being said, most custody situations stay in place until the children turn 18 or finish post-secondary education."

"My friend's 14-year-old was so hard on her," I said.

"Again, not unusual. In my experience,

children take a lot of their frustration and anger out on the custodial parent. It's not fair, but they do it because they usually feel most secure with the custodial parent and they realize they can vent their frustrations without jeopardizing that parent's love for them. Relationships with access parents are sometimes less secure, and there's a tendency for children to be on their best behaviour with the access parent. Children often blame themselves for the separation and they don't want to do anything during the access visit to cause that parent not to want to see them again. In my experience, custodial parents receive the brunt of criticism, frustration, and anger. Child psychologists I have spoken with say not to take it personally and to deal with it calmly. But that's easier said than done, I expect."

"Would the court ever separate Kent and Jeff?"

"In unusual circumstances they might. However courts usually like to keep siblings together."

"Will the court speak with the children?" I asked.

"Judges abhor cases where the children are placed in the middle. They disapprove of any parent who wants to put the children on the stand in court. If you want Kent and Jeff's point of view to be brought forward to a court, we can either ask to have the Children's Lawyer appointed, or request a custody and access assessment. A Children's Lawyer, called different things in different states and provinces, is a lawyer appointed by the state who meets with the children and tells the Judge the children's views and preferences."

"Who pays for the Children's Lawyer?"

"The government pays for the Children's Lawyer. Typically that lawyer is only appointed where children are at risk of harm. The government decides whether to become involved on a case by case basis," Nora replied.

"What is a custody and access assessment?"

"A child psychologist, psychiatrist, social worker or other qualified assessor meets with you, your children, Michael, you and the children together, Michael and the children together, and any extended family members. He or she then writes a report making recommendations to the court as to custody and access," Nora explained. "It is paid for by you and Michael, and ranges in price from $1,500 to $10,000."

I began considering bankruptcy court. "Wow!" I exclaimed.

"Will Michael's adultery affect his right to custody?" I asked bitterly.

"No, it won't," Nora replied. "It used to be that if a woman committed adultery, she would lose custody of her children. Fortunately, that law went off the books long ago. Courts look at the best interests of the children. Even if a mother committed adultery with a few men and is now living with one of them, if it's in the children's best interests to live with her, the courts will award her custody."

"What about homosexuality?" I inquired, thinking of Sandy's brother. "Courts would never award custody to a homosexual, would they?"

"On the contrary. Homosexuality is irrelevant to a court unless it affects the best interests of children. Thus, a court would certainly award custody to a woman or man who was homosexual if he or she were the best caregiver for the children and if it were in their best interests to be with that parent. I've had a few clients whose husbands left them to explore their homosexuality. In those cases, courts will continue to allow access to the departing husband. In fact, custody was granted in one such case because the father was the principal caregiver."

"Really!" I figured this news would make Sandy happy.

"I have a friend, Ruth, whose husband never sees the children," I continued. "If there's a court order that he see them, can't she force him to?"

"No," Nora replied. "If an access parent refuses to see his or her children, there is nothing one can do to force him to see them. Sometimes the court will increase child support to offset the babysitting costs incurred. But that's it."

"Ruth's husband had supervised access to the children. Can't I obtain supervised access to Michael to prevent him, say, from fleeing to Massachusetts with them?" I asked.

"Actually, probably not," Nora replied. "Supervised access is only ordered where there is a tangible risk of harm. For example, if the father has never cared for the child before, or has abducted the child before and it's feared he will again or if he has an alcohol or drug abuse problem that is proven to the court. The fact that you believe there's a minimal risk that Michael *may* take the children to Boston is not enough. To allay those fears, the court would probably order that Michael couldn't remove the children from Ontario without your written consent, and would then allow him unsupervised access to his boys."

My mind wandered back to Michael in school. He had been so full of ambition and energy. I had never known anyone like him. So tall, so muscular. I had loved to draw him, naked, sprawled in a tangle of sheets. His trim hips, the slope of his spine, the broad muscular chest. He had a throaty laugh and a twinkle in his eyes.

Coming out of my daydream, I realized that Nora was talking about child support.

"A lot has changed in the last couple of

years," Nora was saying. "Child support is an obligation that every parent has to provide for his or her child. In most of North America, child support payments are now determined by *Child Support Guidelines*. These guidelines look at the payer's income, the payer being the non-custodial or non-principal residence parent. Some states also look at the principal residence parent's income. The courts then make a support order based on income. Tell me again, how much does Michael earn?" Nora asked.

I replied that I thought it was around $100,000 per year.

"Michael is required to provide you with the last three year's income-tax returns and notices of assessment, a recent statement from his employer setting out income this year to date, and financial statements from his business with his sister including a statement of all salaries, wages and management fees that are paid to persons or related corporations. For now, let's assume he earns $100,000 per year. With two children, he would need to pay $1240 per month on that income for the children. If you and Michael were living in Boston, the exact child support payment may vary somewhat"

"Do I have to pay tax on that money?" I asked.

"No. In Canada, any agreement or order

made after May 1, 1997 is net of taxes, meaning that the $1240 per month would be after-tax money; you wouldn't need to pay tax on it and Michael couldn't deduct his payments from his income. In the United States, it depends on where you live whether you have to claim child support as income."

"Does Michael have any say over how I might use that money?" I asked.

"No. Support is paid to you and you spend it on yourself and the children at your discretion."

"I should tell Ruth that she no longer needs to pay tax on her child support as of May 1st," I exclaimed. Sandy had told me that Ruth paid taxes every year on child support.

"Not so fast, Sam," Nora warned. "In Canada, court orders and agreements made prior to May 1, 1997 are still taxable to the recipient and deductible by the payer, in that case Ruth and her ex-husband respectively. If Ruth wants her child support to be net of taxes, she would need to bring a court application requesting that, assuming her ex-husband didn't agree."

"When does child support end?" I asked.

"Child support continues so long as the child is unable, by reason of illness, disability or other cause, to withdraw from your care or obtain the necessaries of life. In English, this means you will receive child support for Kent and Jeff so long as they are enrolled in school full-time and generally until they receive their college or university degree or diploma."

"Wow. So I should encourage Kent to pursue medicine?" I laughed.

"No. Courts have generally determined that the non-custodial parent must continue support until the children receive their first degree or diploma, or until they quit full-time school. After that, the child is on its own! This time limit is always subject to revision at a judge's discretion, and there have been a few cases recently where principal-residence parents are entitled to child support after the child achieves his first degree and is continuing to one year of teacher's college, but that is not yet the norm."

"There are a few factors that may change the guideline amount of support payable," Nora continued. "For example, if Michael spends more than 40% of time with the children, he can ask a court to vary his child support payable. The court will then consider the increased costs of shared custody arrangements and the conditions, means, needs and other circumstances of the spouses. Courts will often decrease his child support if he spends more than 40% of his time with the children."

"Can Michael claim that because he is now supporting Jennifer, he can't pay me as much child support as the guidelines say he should?" I queried.

Nora replied, "the only way to decrease his child support obligation, short of spending 40% of time with the children, is for him to convince a court he's under undue hardship. Undue hardship means that Michael is responsible for an unusually high level of debts reasonably incurred to support you and the children prior to the marriage breakdown, or that he has a legal duty under an order or agreement to support another person, or has a legal duty to support a disabled child, former spouse or parent. Otherwise, Michael will be paying guideline support. His new relationship is irrelevant."

"What about Kent and Jeff's after-school daycare programs?"

"Michael will have to pay part of that expense. The court calls this sort of expense an 'add-on'. Add-ons affect special or extraordinary expenses for the children. They are limited to childcare expenses, including daycare or nanny costs, extraordinary medical or health-related expenses, extraordinary private-school expenses or other educational programs that meet the child's needs, expenses for post-secondary education, and extraordinary expenses for extracurricular activities. Courts consider whether the expense is necessary and reasonable considering the child's best interests and the patterns of your spending on the children prior to separation."

"Their after-school daycare costs $600 per month. Will Michael have to pay all of it?" I enquired.

"No. Michael will have to pay a proportion of this expense in accordance with your two incomes. The total amount paid will be reduced by tax deductions that will be available to you, such as childcare deductions on your income tax return."

"So, Michael will have to pay about $1240 per month plus a proportion of their daycare expenses?"

"That's right."

"So, I want sole custody. I want Michael to have generous access. And I want child support."

"That's right. In addition, there are spousal support payments owing from Michael to you as we discussed last time."

I asked Nora, "what if I want to change Kent and Jeff's surnames to my maiden name?"

"Well, you can change your own surname back to your maiden name at any time. You may only need to show your birth certificate, or you may need to pay a small fee to the appropriate government office and explain why you want to change it back. But the children's names generally require you to give Michael at minimum notice of your desire to change them, and in some states and provinces, require his consent."

"I doubt he'd consent, Nora. Is there any other way?" I inquired.

"Yes, Sam. You could use your maiden name as one of their names at common law, meaning that their legal names would stay the same as Michael's, but you could add your own name in the middle or at the end when registering them in school and that sort of thing. Of course, Michael could ask a judge to make you stop doing that if he found out. The other option is you could go to court and ask a court to allow you to change their names. Most judges will opt to maintain the children's pre-separation names unless you can show that the change of name is in their best interests."

I decided to forget about changing their names for now, although I vowed to march into the bank this afternoon with my birth certificate to change my own name. No more Mrs. Campbell for me. I was going back to Hadley. Ms. Hadley. That had a nice ring to it, I thought. Considering my new independence, I also wondered if I could relocate with the children to begin my life afresh.

"Nora, what if I wanted to move with the boys to California?" I asked. "For example, what if I married a movie star or something," I said with a smile.

"Mobility is a very difficult issue in any separation or divorce," she replied. "It's up to a judge to balance the best interests of the children, considering your reason for leaving and your plans in the new place on the one hand, and considering the status quo on the other. All such decisions are predicated on what the court perceives as the best interests of the children."

"But surely they wouldn't make me stay here if my new husband lived in California?"

"They won't make you stay, but they may make the children stay," Nora replied.

"That seems unfair," I objected.

"Yes, to you. But imagine how Michael would feel if the children were moved away. As I said, Sam, it's a difficult issue for courts to deal with and typically they have to make a decision where one parent wins and the other loses. But let's not worry about that until we have to, okay," Nora continued. "Unless you have something to tell me..." she smiled.

"Yes, Nora, Kevin Costner just broke up with his wife and asked me to marry him," I teased.

"Did he send you a message in a bottle then?" Nora played along. I laughed.

"Back on topic, what about travelling with the children?" I asked. "What if I wanted to take them to California to meet Kevin?"

"Your parenting plan or court order will provide for obtaining passports for the children and transferring birth certificates back and forth as needed. It may also require each parent's written consent before you can travel with the children."

"So, I want sole custody, generous access to Michael, support for the boys and support for myself," I summarized.

"Exactly, Sam," Nora confirmed. "You're a quick study!" We booked another appointment for next week, and I left with another to-do list.

---

The next day I met with Dr. Morton who began our session discussing children.

"You've done a good job in minimizing the impact of separation on your children," he began. "A lot of my clients forget that the children are in the middle, even though they had no say over the separation. It's critical for parents to minimize the impact of the event on their children."

"I find that so difficult," I replied. "Kent and Jeff are bright, and they pick up on my feelings. When I'm depressed, Jeff becomes withdrawn and Kent tries to mother me."

Dr. Morton cautioned, "it's not unusual for children to try to 'take care of' their parents. But it's not healthy for them to feel the need to parent their parents and it's important that you are here working through things with me to avoid placing unfair burdens on them."

I began to cry. I felt so awful that the children were in the middle.

"Sam, it's healthy to cry, but don't crucify yourself over this. Kids are bright. They understand what is going on no matter what you tell them. Your only objective is to try to keep them out of the middle of the dispute between you and Michael. Kids become insecure when their parents divorce. They lose part of their identity. Think about when you were a child. Your whole life was your parents. And when your dad died, how did you feel?"

Again, I thought back and the memories came flooding in, vividly. "I felt abandoned. I felt I needed to care for my mother." I was starting to understand Dr. Morton's comments. That must be how Kent and Jeff felt. "How can I help them?" I asked Dr. Morton.

"Children typically go through similar feelings to you. They may initially be upset and probably protest, denying that this is happening to them. They may withdraw and become sad, depressed and despondent. Finally, they will come to accept your separation. The key, Sam, is to be open with them and listen to them. Don't expect them to be chipper all the time. Let them take time to deal with this. Kent and Jeff's ability to cope with the separation depends on your communicating with them and providing stability and security. Listen when they talk, and try to reduce any conflict around them.

I resolved there and then to go home and lavish them with my attention that evening. I would turn off the television and listen to them, listen to their feelings. I had been so caught up in my own shock and depression that I'd been ignoring them a bit.

"Kent and Jeff will come through the separation intact," Dr. Morton continued. "You and Michael have already fostered a healthy self-image in both of them, and they seem able to love and be loved. They'll be fine."

I felt a lot better listening to Dr. Morton. It was becoming clearer to me what the boys must be going through.

"How did telling them about the separation go?" Dr. Morton asked.

"It was the most difficult discussion I've ever had with them," I replied. "But they were stoic and after I reassured them it was not their fault and their lives wouldn't change, they seemed okay." It was obvious how relieved I was.

"There are a number of things you should not do to Kent and Jeff. First of all, never use the children as spies on Michael. They should be spared having to take sides in your separation, and should not feel that they need to be disloyal to one parent to satisfy the other parent's curiosity."

I had not thought of having them spy. Actually, they could relay a lot of information about Michael to me, I realized. But Dr. Morton was probably right. It would make them miserable having to report on their father. Oh well, that's what friends and private investigators are for. I chuckled quietly; picturing Sandy parked outside of Michael's door monitoring his every movement for me. How pathetic I thought.

Dr. Morton looked at me quizzically.

"Oh, it's nothing, Doctor. Just plotting how to make Michael's life miserable. It's become quite a preoccupation lately." I smiled and shrugged.

"That's not unusual, Sam. Just try to keep the children out of the middle." He smiled back. I wondered if Dr. Morton was married or single.

"Answer the boys' questions calmly and as honestly as is appropriate. Your highest priority is to keep their lives as stable as possible. That means don't fight with Michael in front of them. Keep their exposure to tension and conflict low. And keep their lives normal, stable, as ordinary as possible."

I thought of Kent and Jeff's reaction when they knew their father wasn't returning. They were shocked. I realized now their sense of security, of stability, of self was threatened. We, their primary caregivers, were throwing them quite a curve ball.

My session with Dr. Morton flew by, and

before I knew it, it was time to go.

# 5

## STEP FOUR:
## TAKE HALF THE CASH

Nora and I had an appointment on Wednesday.

"Hi, Sam. How was your week?" She enquired.

"Lousy. I forgot to tell you last time, but I told the boys about the separation on my own, Michael came over and insulted me, and I cried more than I have in years. But I managed to complete a beautiful polar bear," I rambled.

"A polar bear?" she enquired, clearly confused.

"Yes, I painted a polar bear," I explained. "An angry polar bear!"

She laughed. "Things become easier with time. You're going to have to trust me on that."

I'll believe it when it happens, I thought.

On the agenda for today's meeting were money issues and property division.

She began immediately. "Separation will cost you money. You may need to pay for new accommodation, and will need to pay legal bills."

I already knew about legal bills. Nora had required a $1000 retainer, which I had paid by credit card.

"You may need to survive a few months without support from Michael. Ideally you and Michael will discuss your and the children's financial needs and enter into an interim agreement to meet those needs. But if you are concerned Michael will clean out the joint accounts, it's important that you immediately take half the cash."

"I was wondering how I was going to survive while Michael and I negotiated an agreement," I stated. "Michael has so far kept depositing his pay cheque into our joint account and I assume the household bills are being paid from that."

"Excellent. I discussed that with his lawyer and it appears he will continue to make these deposits while we negotiate," Nora confirmed.
"Have you borrowed the books I recommended on money management from the library yet?" She asked.

"Not yet, Nora, but I'm on a waiting list for *The Millionaire Next Door*," I advised.

"A lot of my clients find money management baffling. Many of them have never managed money before," Nora continued. "Are you comfortable balancing your chequebook, Sam, or investing and saving money?"

"I've never done it in my life. Michael had always been so good with numbers that I had never bothered to learn."

"I recommend that you attend a few financial

planning seminars to learn the basics. Don't buy anything at these seminars - just gather information."

I wrote this on my to-do list.

"You'll need to set a budget for the year, and set financial goals and objectives. For example, you'll need to start setting aside some money for the boys' post-secondary educational costs."

I had recently read a staggering article claiming that an education for Kent and Jeff, by the time they were old enough, would cost in the six-figure area. How I was ever going to save this amount of money was beyond me.

"You'll need money to pay me." Nora said. "Furthermore you will need to set aside some money, an emergency fund if you will, to tide you over if Michael refuses to pay support one month or bounces a cheque. You may also need money for moving expenses if you can't keep the house."

I hadn't thought of all the money I was going to need. I began to panic. "Where do I find all this money?" I asked worriedly.

"I always recommend that my clients take half of the cash available in joint bank accounts and joint investments. If your spouse is reasonable, you and he can agree to this and divide the amounts there. If you assume Michael will instead want to take it all, though, I recommend you take half of it immediately. Put it in your own name so you control it, and let Michael know after the fact that you took half of the cash and explain why."

I could imagine Michael's reaction to my taking half of the cash. But I understood very clearly why Nora suggested it. I was going to need a lot of money in the next few months and could only rely upon myself.

"Another thing, Sam. This may sound sneaky and underhanded, but if you haven't already done so, you should finish photocopying for me every financial document in the house before Michael removes them. This may not be necessary, but it's a safeguard if he refuses to disclose where his bank accounts and your joint investments are. Given that Michael controlled the money, the more you can find out now about the location of investments, the more confident I will be that we know where everything is."

I hadn't yet completed this. I could imagine myself sneaking around my own house trying to dig up Michael's financial documents. Sandy and I had started the process after our first meeting with Nora, but were unable to find anything financial. Michael may have already taken them, I thought. I would find out that evening, I vowed. "I'll feel a little funny doing this," I explained to Nora. "But I do want to ensure I know where our money is. I'll do it tonight."

Michael and I had started with nothing.

When my dad died, he left me $100,000 in trust which was managed by my mother until I was 30 years old. She hadn't advanced any money to us at the beginning. Michael's mom had nothing.

Michael had insisted, once he obtained employment with Finney and Wallace that we purchase a home. We chose one close to the lake. It cost $100,000 in 1986 and I loved it there. When Michael was promoted, he had wanted to move into something bigger, maybe in Bloor West Village, but I had wanted to stay put. I had a tiny studio off the kitchen that I adored, and the kids liked their school. Our backyard was fairly large with a swingset and fort for Kent and Jeff. In the evening, the smell of moist earth, leaves and bark drifted in. It was a cool, familiar comfort.

I was glad I had insisted on staying put. The boys and I would be comfortable in that house. And hopefully I could afford it.

"Samantha, you seemed a bit lost. Can I get you some water or something?" Nora enquired.

"No, I'm fine. You were discussing money."

"Yes. Specifically property division. First, there are some misconceptions out there that I'd like to clear up," Nora began. "Some people think that the minute you marry, you are entitled to half of the other person's property. That's generally not true. So, for example, if you had $100,000 on the date of marriage, and Michael had nothing, he would not be entitled to half of your money by virtue of marrying."

I had been worried about my trust fund. "So he is not entitled to the trust fund I had when we married," I confirmed.

"That's right, Sam," Nora said. "If the $100,000 were in the family residence on date of marriage, you may owe him half of the value, but a trust fund you owned then is all yours."

"What if I had owned this house on date of marriage. Would Michael be entitled to half of it?" I asked.

"In a lot of provinces and states, yes," Nora replied. "In your case, a trust fund is not shareable. But if you had owned a home, you would have been wise to obtain a marriage contract."

"What's a marriage contract?" I asked.

"We'll discuss that later. For our purposes now, you just need to understand that marriage in itself doesn't create ownership in property. So, Sam, what did you have when you married?"

"A $100,000 trust fund controlled by my mother, and a beat-up Datsun," I replied.

"And Michael?"

"He had student loans of $10,000."

"Okay. And what do you own today?"

"Well, we own our house although there's a mortgage. Michael has Registered Retirement Savings Plans and opened a spousal Registered

Retirement Savings Plan for me. We have some bonds and a bit of savings. Michael owns a cottage with his sister that we use every summer. And he owns half of the landscaping business with his sister. Our cars are leased, and I think that's it. Here, I've written down the assets I'm aware of." I handed Nora my figures.

| Assets and Debts | |
|---|---|
| House | 200,000 |
| Mortgage | 50,000 |
| Trust Fund | 100,000 |
| Registered Retirement Savings Plan | 60,000 |
| Spousal Plan | 10,000 |
| Bonds and Savings | 5,000 |
| Cottage Michael owns with sister | 100,000 |
| Michael's business with sister | 40,000 |

"Okay. So the Etobicoke house is worth $200,000 with a $50,000 mortgage? You still have your trust fund worth $100,000. Yes, and his Registered Retirement Savings Plans are worth about $60,000 you figure. The spousal Registered Retirement Savings Plan is worth $10,000, the bonds and savings $5,000. What do you figure his cottage is worth?"

"I don't know. Probably $100,000. His business employs his sister full-time and last year had revenues of about $90,000. Michael mentioned a while ago that someone in Massachusetts was interested in purchasing it, but would only offer $40,000."

"All right. Now, when you divide property in North America, the increase in value of a couple's assets during marriage is divided equally between them. Let me show you how that works:

|  | Sam | Michael |
|---|---|---|
| **_Date of Marriage_** | | |
| Trust Fund | 100,000 | |
| Datsun | 2,000 | |
| Student Loans | | (10,000) |
| | 102,000 | (10,000) |
| | | |
| **_Date of Separation_** | | |
| House | 100,000 | 100,000 |
| Mortgage | (25,000) | (25,000) |
| Trust Fund | 100,000 | |
| Registered Retirement Savings Plan | 10,000 | 60,000 |
| Bonds and Savings | 2,500 | 2,500 |
| Cottage (Michael's half) | | 50,000 |
| Business (Michael's half) | | 20,000 |
| | 187,500 | 207,500 |
| | | |
| Increase in net worth | 85,500 | 217,500 |
| | | |
| Difference | | 132,000 |
| | | |
| Michael owes Sam | | 66,000 |

"At date of marriage, you were worth $102,000 and Michael had a net worth of negative $10,000. Today, Michael is worth $207,500 and you are worth $187,500. So, your net worth during marriage increased by $85,500 and Michael's net worth increased by $217,500. In Ontario, Michael would owe you about $66,000 so Michael's increase in net worth would be reduced to $151,500 and your increase would be raised to the same, $151,500. Other provinces and states calculate the amount owing somewhat differently, but all are similar."

Nora wrote all of this down on a piece of paper so I could better understand it.

"So," Nora repeated, "because Michael has more assets than you do and because his increase in property has been greater than yours during the marriage, he owes you $66,000 so that both of your increases in value will total $151,500."

"So, I need to sell the house to divide it equally, sell the bonds to divide them equally, and in addition, Michael owes me $66,000?" I asked.

"Basically, that's accurate. Now, as we discussed, if you want to remain in the house with Kent and Jeff, you will probably have to buy Michael's half from him at a price you agree upon, if you can agree. You would then offset the $66,000 owing from Michael against his $75,000 equity in the home. You would have to ask the bank to arrange to transfer the mortgage into your name alone and the home would be transferred to you."

"So, basically I would end up with the home and Michael would end up with his Registered Retirement Savings Plans?"

"Yes. That's not at all uncommon in family-law settlements," Nora replied.

"But we're forgetting about his adultery," I stated, indignant. "I didn't want the marriage to end. Why should I have to divide the property equally when it was he who walked out?"

"Unfortunately, conduct is usually irrelevant when dividing property." Nora explained. "There are a few circumstances where conduct would matter, such as if Michael recklessly depleted family assets or falsely gifted third parties, like his sister, to avoid paying you equalization; or if equal division would be unconscionable or inequitable. Things like that may affect equalization. I don't think any of these apply to you, do they Sam?"

"No," I agreed. "Do I have to share my trust fund with Michael?"

"No. Because you had your trust fund on date of marriage and because it pays out the interest income to you every year, you don't need to share your trust fund. If you had been given the trust fund after you were married, it would be excluded from sharing as well, so long as it was given to you alone and you didn't put it under joint names or into the matrimonial home."

"Michael received $10,000 from his great-aunt when she died, and I think he put that money into building our porch. Does he get that money back?"

"No, Sam. That money has been spent and is not in existence on date of separation. He cannot claim it back."

"What about his business? How do I know the value of his business?" I asked.

"For our purposes, I have used the fair market value of the business based on the amount offered to him for it. Half of that value is Michael's if he's a half owner. We could argue that because he didn't sell it for that amount, it has a higher value to him. We would need a business valuator to calculate its value. Unfortunately, this usually costs $2,500 or more. So unless the business is worth a fair amount of money, it doesn't make sense to value it. I would recommend you use $40,000 if he was offered that, or something close to that number for equalization purposes, unless you think for some reason it has dramatically increased in value in the last couple of years since the offer was made."

"I'll think about that," I said. "What about his pension?" I inquired. "Aren't I entitled to half of it?"

"It depends on the sort of pension he has. Does Michael have a pension at work?" Nora asked.

"No, they just help him with his Registered Retirement Savings Plan contributions," I replied.

"In that case, there's no value to the pension other than the value of the Registered Retirement Savings Plans. But in some cases, Sam, there are pensions available to employees and those pensions must be valued by an actuary to determine their value to the spouse. Adding up the contributions of the employee and employer is insufficient. Typically pensions for family-law purposes have a higher value than the sum of the contributions. I have a lot of clients who work for the Board of Education, and they have defined-benefit pension plans that promise to pay them a certain monthly amount upon retirement. Those sorts of pensions must be valued. However what we call a money-purchase pension can usually be valued like a Registered Retirement Savings Plan, just by finding out how much is in it."

"But if a couple only has a pension and no other assets, how is that amount paid?" I asked.

"The courts have significant discretion in ordering payment of a pension. They can order that the spouse divides the pension when and if it is received, or they can order that the pension holder pay the other spouse installment payments over a number of years. Most commonly, though, they order it paid as a lump sum immediately, which means the one spouse may have to borrow money to pay the amount owing to the other spouse if there are no other assets."

"Wow! That seems really unfair," I exclaimed.

"Some people feel it is unfair, although the courts and the legislature have decided that a pension is a valuable asset and should be valued accordingly. If the parties had stayed together, the other spouse would benefit from the pension, so the courts feel that he or she should still benefit in some way. You are also entitled to divide Michael's Canada Pension Plan," Nora continued.

"Nora, I'm only 34!" I teased. "Are you trying to age me more this month than I have already?"

"No, no, Sam, I just want you to know," Nora smiled. "Canada Pension Plan credits are equally divided between spouses if their divorce became final after January 1, 1987. You can apply at any time, Sam, and Michael cannot stop you. The law in the United States is similar."

"What if I wanted to stay in the house for the next ten years and not divide property until after?" I asked.

"Courts are able to award what we call exclusive possession of the matrimonial home if you wanted this, but I doubt in your case they would. You and Michael have enough monies to divide property now, and there's no reason a court would make Michael wait for his money from the house until ten years had elapsed. Also, you need to keep in mind that there are limitation periods. You can't wait forever to apply for division of property," Nora concluded.

"So, to re-cap, Nora. I'm entitled to half of the increase in value of our property during marriage. All property is valued as of the date of separation, being April 14, 1997. I'm able to deduct my trust fund from my assets because I owned it on the date of marriage. Michael must add his student loans to his increased property today because he owed them on date of marriage. Everything else is divided equally, and because Michael has more investments than I do, he will owe me $66,000 in equalization. Have I covered everything?"

"Almost. There are some adjustments that may come into play when you and Michael are negotiating your agreement. For example, if you're going to keep the home, the court will probably let you deduct some money for real estate commission and legal fees even though these expenses won't actually be incurred yet. Or the court will probably let Michael deduct some money for taxes that he would have to pay if he liquidated his Registered

Retirement Savings Plan."

By this time, I was becoming tired. All this new information was swimming in my head. "Nora, I'm exhausted. I'm not sure that I'm taking all of this in."

"That's normal, Sam. Take a break for lunch, and we'll continue our meeting after you've eaten. I'm going to give you a financial statement in draft that you can begin filling out, and we'll meet next Friday morning to review the statement."

Looking over the financial statement, I became disheartened. "I hate budgeting, Nora. This financial statement looks complicated."

"It is kind of complicated. Just do your best and you and I will complete the rest. Okay."

"Okay. See you after lunch."

Even though I was exhausted, I felt a lot better than I had a week ago. Nora's words and information had reassured me. I felt better already eating. At least now I understood my basic legal rights. I figured I could review all information with Sandy before next Friday. In the meantime, Nora had more to tell me that afternoon.

# 6

## STEP FIVE: CONSIDER MEDIATION

The food really picked me up.

Nora began immediately. "Where did we finish before lunch? I think I was about to explain the many options you have," she began. "There are three ways to proceed with Michael. The first is called agreement or negotiation. It means that you and Michael enter into a contract setting out all the terms that you have agreed to."

"We'll never agree. He wants the boys one week of every two," I scoffed.

"Don't be so quick to assume you won't agree. Of all my cases, approximately only 1% ever go to trial. All the rest settle at some point, whether before starting a court action, through mediation or negotiation or just before trial. You're getting ahead of yourself however. Let's talk about agreement for a moment. Family-law lawyers are often able to negotiate a settlement. Thus, once we complete your financial statement and Michael completes his, I should be able to give you an opinion on what I think a judge would order in this case fairly accurately. If Michael has a lawyer who does as much family law as I do, our respective assessments should be reasonably similar. If his lawyer and I talk and negotiate, we should be able to finish this matter and draft up a separation agreement for both your and Michael's benefit."

"What if you and Michael's lawyer disagree?"

"At any rate we should be able to narrow the issues in dispute to one or two. In your case it may be spousal support. In that situation, you and I would proceed to court for an order for interim spousal support. Such an order would give both myself and Michael's lawyer a good idea of what a judge would do with spousal support at trial. Probably after that, we could negotiate a final agreement incorporating the terms of spousal support determined by a judge."

"I hope we can reach agreement," I said. "Everything I read says court is expensive."

"Negotiation is definitely the cheapest method of settling your differences with Michael. If you and Michael can communicate, the two of you could come to some sort of tentative arrangement that we could put into a separation agreement."

"Michael and I are not talking," I stated firmly.

"That is not unusual, at least initially. There's a lot of hurt and anger between you now. That's why an objective lawyer is helpful at this point. Down the road, who knows? You may find you're able to communicate better regarding the children than you did during the marriage. So, negotiation is your first option."

"What if that doesn't work?" I asked.

"If negotiation is unsuccessful, or if you feel you and Michael could settle things yourself with a bit of help, you may want to attend mediation. That's where both of you sit down, with or without your lawyers - your choice - and a mediator tries to reach agreement between you."

"That sounds intimidating." I could just picture Michael screaming at me over the table in front of the mediator telling him what a lousy person I was.

"Mediation is actually an extremely friendly process. You and Michael must be calm and must discuss your differences with a view to reaching an agreement in the best interests of the children."

That didn't sound so bad.

"There are two types of mediation," Nora continued. "The first, closed mediation, means that anything you say in mediation is confidential and that the mediator cannot testify in court about what was said. The second, open mediation, means that whatever you say can be used and the mediator can testify in court. You and I can discuss which type is best for you."

"Where do I find a mediator?"

"We can provide you with names, as can the local law society or bar association. There are some listed in the phone book. There is currently no registration or regulation of mediators, so it's always a good idea to find one through a reputable source, such as your lawyer."

"How expensive is mediation?"

"Mediators usually charge between $100 and $200 per hour. But considering you and Michael would be sharing the costs instead of each paying a lawyer, it's almost always much cheaper."

"Does a mediator have to be a lawyer?" I queried.

"No, in fact, it can be anyone. Often it is a psychologist when the issues are child-focussed, other times it's a health professional. It can be anyone whose judgment you trust and with whom you are comfortable."

"So a Catholic priest could mediate?" I asked.

"Yes, Sam. It can be anyone whom you both trust, although for a mediator to be productive the mediator should have experience resolving disputes and reconciling differing interests. In mediation you and Michael sit down with a person, be it a lawyer or a psychologist or health professional or priest, and the three of you try to agree on some of the difficulties confronting you."

"What sorts of difficulties?" I asked.

"For example, you could discuss a parenting plan for Kent and Jeff and decide who will make decisions about education, religion and health. You would discuss what time-sharing arrangement would be best for the children. Or what their extra-curricular activities should be and how much money was needed for ballet lessons, skiing lessons and daycare."

"Would you be with me?" I asked.

"I could be with you, although it's not necessary," Nora responded. "If you opt to mediate, you and I can discuss the issues you want to try to agree upon prior to your attending mediation and your legal position if the matter should go to trial."

"What about money? Could we discuss money at mediation?"

"You can discuss anything that you need to be resolved. For a mediator to address money and equalization issues he or she would need to have a fundamental understanding of family-law issues. In that case, he or she should probably be a family-law lawyer or former judge."

"What if mediation doesn't work?" I pressed.

"If neither mediation nor negotiation works you have two choices. You can either arbitrate or litigate. Arbitration means that you and Michael, usually through your lawyers, choose someone to listen to both sides of the story and make a binding decision. You and Michael would pay for that person's time. Usually that person is a family-law lawyer or a former family-law judge. He or she would make a final decision regarding you, Michael and the children."

"Sounds pretty terrifying," I said.

"Your other option is litigation. Sometimes, initially, it's crucial that you litigate to establish your right to interim spousal support or to establish the principal residence for the children if it is contested. That means you and I would draft a document which would be filed in court and a date for a court appearance would be set."

"Would Michael know about it?" I asked.

"Yes. Once the proceeding was issued, Michael would be personally served with a copy and you and I would swear statements for the court to read, asking for interim relief. Interim means temporary, or to last until the trial or final settlement."

"Would the judge want me to testify?" I asked, concerned.

"Generally not at the interim stage. You would swear an affidavit to support your request of the court, and Michael would swear one in response. The judge would read both affidavits and would then make a decision about whatever issues were in front of him or her," Nora explained. "You could apply for interim custody, interim access, interim sale of the matrimonial home, an interim restraining order, interim spousal support or child support, interim payments or interim exclusive possession. Almost anything you could obtain at a trial you can obtain on an interim basis."

This sounded confusing.

"Once the interim order is made, it lasts until another order is made, a trial occurs, or a settlement is reached," Nora continued.

"Does a judge ever meet Michael and me?" I asked.

"Generally at the case conference, sometimes called a pre-trial. At court, you sit down with your lawyer, Michael and Michael's lawyer. A judge will tell you what he or she would do with this case if it were presented for trial. This encourages settlement because judges are the ones who will eventually hear these matters, and their opinion is very important."

"Are judges as intimidating in person as on television?" I asked, thinking of Judge Judy.

"Judges are generally very nice people, but often stern. They're a great help in settling matters however," Nora explained.

"What if Michael wouldn't agree at that stage?" I asked.

"If a pre-trial didn't settle the matter, you would usually go to discovery. Discovery is an out of court process, under oath, at an official examiner's office. There I would cross-examine Michael and his lawyer would cross-examine you. We would exchange any documents that were needed or required, and would prepare for trial."

Trial. What a frightening thought!

"Litigation ends with a trial. There, you would have to give evidence, as would Michael. Any valuators you used or other experts you needed would also testify. A judge would listen to all of the evidence and would then make a final order."

"Wow. That sounds expensive!" I was sure I couldn't afford it.

"It can be very expensive to litigate a case all the way to trial. An interim court proceeding usually costs $2000 to $25,000, depending on how contested it is, and it can be a great help in moving past Michael's stubbornness, if needed. Cases usually settle after the interim court hearing. A full-blown custody and property trial could easily cost anywhere from $20,000 to $200,000."

"Maybe I should give up and give Michael the boys," I said dispiritedly.

"Don't be silly, Sam. I've told you the worst-case scenario. Do you remember how many matters actually go to trial?" Nora prodded.

"Ten percent?" I felt badly. I hadn't been listening.

"One percent. No more. For now let's focus

on how you and I want to proceed. Michael's lawyer has contacted me. He seems like a nice fellow although I've never dealt with him before. He and I have agreed to exchange your financial statements in the next month. In the meantime, you and I should draft an interim agreement dealing with custody and access. What I suggest we do is set out that you have principal residence of the children and Michael has them on alternate weekends. Is that okay?"

"Yes, I suppose." I wanted a copy of Michael's lawyer's letter. Had it mentioned my drinking? Had it insisted on having the boys one-week of every two?

"Here's a copy of Michael's lawyer's letter. Rod Sterling is his name. His letter advises that Michael has retained him and suggests that we exchange financial statements."

I let out a relieved sigh. Maybe Michael was not going to make good on his threats.

Michael had initially seen the boys every second day, stopping in to say hello to us and taking them for dinner three times a week. That however had quickly tapered off. He now spoke of spending alternate weekends with them, although he hadn't yet done so. He had cancelled last weekend with them. The boys' disappointment was evident, so I was trying hard to pretend to like sports and everything else they needed. Overnight I had become mom and dad.

The boys were wonderful, really, trying their best to understand and not complaining when I told them we didn't have money to do some of the things they used to do. Both boys loved hockey and baseball. Since April 14, I had learned more than I ever thought I would about baseball. And in hockey, "pulling the goalie," meant risking it all when you needed a goal. And "Cooper" meant money. A lot of money. I was trying my best to hand down Jeff's skates to Kent, and to purchase Jeff's skates second-hand. How could I possibly pay for new equipment this year?

Nora again explained that I should avoid litigation if possible, because usually the money and time involved could better be put towards productive, positive things in my life.

Nora and I drafted an interim separation agreement that seemed to protect the boys and I. It provided that Michael continue to deposit his pay cheques into the joint account for the next month until we exchanged financial statements. It said that the boys and I would continue to be covered under his medical and dental benefits at work and that he would keep me as his life insurance beneficiary. It gave me principal residence and Michael access. It seemed to cover everything I needed.

"Can I change the home locks?" I enquired.

"Without Michael's consent, you aren't supposed to, but let me write to his lawyer advising that, for security sake, you'd like to and we'll see how he responds. Any other issues you want to deal with, Sam?"

"No, that should be okay. I'll feel much more secure once that agreement is signed."

Nora asked me what I was up to that weekend. I had no idea. Two boys and no father. I expected I would be busy.

As I came in the door, I noticed that Michael had been by to pick up some of his personal items. The coat closet was half-empty. I felt violated. I immediately called Nora.

"Michael just entered the house without my consent, Nora. Can he do that?" I demanded angrily.

"Until this interim agreement is signed giving you exclusive possession, he can. It is jointly owned by him, so he has a right to enter it unless there is an exclusive-possession agreement or order. I'll write a follow-up letter to his lawyer asking him to respect your and the boys' privacy. In the meantime, make sure anything you don't want him to see is hidden."

Just as I hung up, the phone rang again. "Hello."

"Sam, its Michael. I was by the house to pick up a few things. Hope you don't mind. I would have called ahead but you were out."

Fuming, I told him he shouldn't be in the house without my permission. "Sam, calm down. It's my house too. Anyway, I was wondering if I could have the boys this weekend?"

My mind went careening over all the information Nora had given me. What had she said about custody? I didn't have a custody order or agreement. What if he didn't return them? It was almost 4 p.m. "Michael, I'll call you back, okay. There's another call on the line."

Frantically, I dialed Nora's number. I expected I would soon know it by heart.

"Sure, Sam, you can give him the boys this weekend. Just have him sign something agreeing to return them on Sunday night and we should be fine."

Although a little nervous, I called Michael back. "My lawyer says you can have them if you sign a paper saying you'll return them to me Sunday night."

"Fine, Sam. Whatever. If you don't trust me, that's fine. You write it up and I'll sign it when I pick them up. Okay?" He sounded exasperated and insulted. Trust him? Of course I no longer trusted him. The trust had disappeared when he walked out the door and told me I no longer met his needs.

A weekend alone. I couldn't remember the

last time I'd been without the boys and Michael. It had surely been before we were married. I called Sandy. She wasn't home.

When I picked the boys up, I told them they would be seeing their dad this weekend. "Cool," Kent replied. Jeff seemed more hesitant. "It's okay, pumpkin," I reassured. "He'll bring you back Sunday afternoon, and I'm sure you'll have a wonderful time. Okay?" Reassured by my encouragement, Jeff smiled.

At 6 p.m. Michael arrived. Jennifer was nowhere to be seen. Smart man, I thought. I showed him the paper, he signed it, I kissed the boys, and they were gone.

I had a blissful weekend. I took a long bath, went to see a movie with Sandy, and relaxed.

When they returned Sunday, I invited Michael in. It was his house, he had reminded me, yet he let me invite him in. He sat on the couch and I brought him a drink of orange juice.

"Michael, my lawyer has been discussing mediation with me," I began. "Yeah, so has mine," he replied, "he asked me if I had ever hit you. I said no. He asked if you and I could communicate all right. I said yes. He asked if either of us had emotional or mental problems, or if there had ever been physical or sexual abuse. I said no. He then told me the best method of resolving our dispute was probably mediation."

I let out a sigh of relief. Mediation wouldn't cost me $200,000. Whew. "I think we should try it," I concurred.

"Okay, Sam, why don't you talk with your lawyer and we'll meet with the mediator she suggests and see if the process works," he replied.

Michael seemed tired. That sparkle in his eye that I remembered was non-existent. Maybe it was the hour. After all, it was after 10 p.m. Yet he didn't seem happy. Maybe I was deluding myself. I was grasping for false hope, perhaps. I smiled at Michael and offered him more orange juice.

"No thanks, Sam. I'm tired. [I was right!] I should probably be heading to the apartment," he answered. "Good night."

Was it just me, or had he been about to kiss me? I shook my head hard after he left and told myself I couldn't be thinking like this, torturing myself this way. It was over. Remember, Sam, you no longer meet his needs.

Nora set us up with Mary Wong as a mediator. We met with her a few days later. To begin she had both of us discuss the history of our marriage and the outstanding issues as we saw them.

Mary stated, "you both need to compromise. You need to realize that if you dig your heels in and insist on your own way on all issues, you'll end up in court spending a fortune. To reach agreement,

Sam and Michael, you need to use the creative energy you had when you both had the boys and parented them. You need to remember that if you compromise on one issue, the other person may compromise on the next. Keep an open mind to each other and to each other's comments or demands. Try to listen to each other and focus on your children. If you're able to do that, you'll reach a mediated agreement that's in the best interests of your children."

I was comforted by Mary's comments, as was Michael. "Okay, Mary, I'm prepared to try to do what you say," I stated, looking at Michael.

"Me too," he said.

"First of all, we'll work on a parenting plan," Mary continued. "Once you know where the children will be, you can better determine support and property division, including division of the house."

"Okay." Mediation was a good option.

# 7

## STEP SIX:
## MAKE IT ENFORCEABLE

At our next appointment, Nora told me that whatever Michael and I agreed to was fine so long as she put it in writing.

"Why do you need to put it in writing?" I asked. "Why couldn't I go to Grand and Toy and buy a do-it-yourself separation agreement."

"It's critical that whatever you and Michael agree to be enforceable," Nora explained. "If you verbally agree to something and then, a year from now, Michael remarries and decides not to honour it, what will you do?" Nora asked.

"Well, I'd come and see you to make him honour his agreement."

"Why not just do it properly the first time?" She asked with a smile. "Another example. If you prepare a do-it-yourself separation agreement and don't do it properly, what will you do?"

"Okay, Nora, again I would come to you to fix it. And again, you'll ask why I didn't do it properly the first time around. I see what you mean," I replied.

Nora smiled. "It's more than worth your while to have the agreement drafted properly. That way it can be enforced."

"What does 'enforce' mean?" I asked, confused.

"If you have a separation agreement mandating payment of support, for example, and Michael stops providing you with cheques a year from now, you would need to enforce it," Nora explained.

Suddenly concerned, I asked "but what specifically would we do if he stopped voluntarily paying?"

"We would register it with the courts and the government enforcement agency would garnish his pay, Sam," Nora explained. "If that didn't work, we could ask the sheriff to begin selling Michael's assets to pay the monies owing."

"Is that easy, Nora?" I asked.

"No, Sam. Enforcing monies owing is very difficult. It requires persistence, tenacity, and a bit of luck. Eventually you generally recover the monies owing, along with your costs and out-of-pocket expenses," Nora reassured. "Another example of enforcement is custody and access enforcement."

"When would you need that?"

"For example, if Michael picked up Kent and Jeff for an access visit and didn't return them but took them to his mother in Boston, a properly drafted agreement will ensure their return quicker than a verbal agreement or improper do-it-yourself agreement."

"How?"

"You would immediately go to court, advise the judge what happened, and obtain a custody order on the basis of the separation agreement. You would then dispatch the Boston police to pick up the boys and return them to Toronto," Nora explained.

"Obviously you would be an emotional mess and perhaps it would take a while to retrieve the boys. Alternatively you could go with a copy of your separation agreement and pick the boys up yourself."

"Would I be better off with a court order?"

Nora told me, "a properly drafted separation agreement is almost as good as a court order, Sam. A court order means that a judge has ordered something. A judge's order can be made with the consent of you and Michael, like a separation agreement incorporated into a court order. If you and Michael agree ahead of time, you can incorporate your agreement into a court order or divorce judgment if need be."

"I think I want a court order, Nora," I stated.

"Sure, Sam. You would certainly want a court order as opposed to only an agreement if Michael moved back to Boston, or to New York, because you'd need to enforce the custody and access provisions and the child support order in the States."

"Why else might I need to enforce the agreement?" I asked.

"If you're going to keep the house and Michael is relinquishing his interest in it, that agreement must be in writing or Michael could decide a year later that he wanted money for his half of the house. Imagine how you'd feel after making a verbal agreement, and counting on that agreement to keep the house, and then have Michael change his mind."

"Given his change of mind about the marriage, I guess nothing is sacred." I replied. "Or I suppose, from his perspective, if I were relinquishing my right to spousal support in exchange for a lump sum of money, Michael would be pretty annoyed if I forgot our agreement a year later."

"Exactly, Sam. It sounds like you've got it now." Nora smiled.

"Gretchen has an interim order. What's that?"

"An interim order usually lasts until a trial is conducted and a final order is made, or until a final agreement is completed and a final order or agreement completed," Nora explained.

"Can orders be changed?" I asked, thinking of the possibility of one of the boys wanting to live with Michael down the road.

"Orders are always subject to variation regarding children, Sam," Nora explained. "The court can even override an agreement if they don't believe it's in the children's best interests."

"You mean if Michael and I agree on something for the children, a Judge could change what we've agreed to?"

"Yes," Nora explained, "although it happens rarely. But judges always have the power to decide what's in the best interests of the children. If you and Michael agree on a regime that will put the children at risk, a judge will not allow it. You don't need to worry about that, Sam. You should just be aware that a judge has the final say."

"Are orders about children the only type that can be overridden by a judge?" I asked.

"No, Sam. Many are subject to variation, depending on the type of order," she continued. "For example, if you and Michael agreed that he didn't need to pay child support, the judge could override your decision and order him to pay child support in the best interests of the children."

"I've heard that a divorce can be denied if child support isn't being paid," I said. "Is that true?"

"Yes, it is. A judge has the power to deny divorce if children's support is not being taken care of. As another example, a Judge could override an agreement if you and Michael agree that your support will end in five years, and in five years you still cannot support yourself. You could ask the Judge to override the agreement and continue spousal support."

"So anything I sign means nothing?" I asked.

"No. Judges usually respect agreements and you will usually be forced to comply with your agreement. The point is that judges have the power to override the agreement if they feel it's unfair, inequitable or unconscionable," Nora stated.

"A friend of mine had the sheriff seize her husband's bank accounts when he didn't pay support. Is that common?"

"Yes, when support owing is not paid. For instance, if Michael refused to pay support and we couldn't garnish his pay or his bank accounts, you can ask the Sheriff to seize property registered in his name, such as his vehicle," Nora explained. "Although the Sheriff will charge you up front before seizing property, this would probably make Michael more interested in paying support if his car were seized."

"He drives a sport-utility vehicle, Nora. He traded in his car once we separated, and the boys say he calls it his 'Chick-mobile'." I explained.

Nora laughed. "When I was younger, a sport-utility vehicle was definitely not considered a

'Chick-mobile'!" she replied. "I always wanted a guy with a convertible myself."

I laughed too. She was right. I had always wanted a guy in a red sports car. A sport-utility vehicle as a Chick-mobile seemed ridiculous. I liked Nora more knowing she wouldn't go for Michael in a sport-utility vehicle.

"What if I wanted to sell the cottage he received from his grandmother?" I asked. "Could I force Michael to sell it if he refused to pay his support?"

"Yes, that's called seizing and selling property. You would register a court document against the property and then ask the sheriff to sell it," Nora said. "Nonetheless so long as Michael is working, the simplest method of collecting support is to garnishee his wages. What that means is his employer deducts the support money off the top of his cheque so he never has a chance to spend it. Most states and provinces have agencies whose sole function is to collect support payments through garnishing pay."

"I read somewhere that some places suspend a person's driver's licence for non-payment of support."

"Yes, Sam, that's also possible in most states and provinces, usually through those same agencies that garnishee support payments, although each province and state is different."

"On the off change Michael were to take off with the children, how would I find him?"

"The Hague Convention empowers police in most Western countries to retrieve and return children. So if Michael were to flee to the United States or England with them, for example, the police would help you track him down and the American or English police would arrest him, take the children from him and fly them back to you," Nora explained.

"Would Michael be jailed when he returned to Canada?" I asked.

"Sometimes. Other times, he might be prevented from seeing the children at all, or might be forced to see them in a supervised setting only. The court has wide discretion in cases like that. Thankfully such cases are rare."

I couldn't imagine Michael fleeing with Kent and Jeff. They were too old. They would wonder where I was. And Kent would probably call me. I was glad they weren't infants.

"On the flip side, Sam, if you refused to allow Michael to see Kent and Jeff despite a court order or agreement, the police could intervene and force the visitation, and Michael could take you to court and ask for you to be jailed for contempt. Again, an unusual penalty, yet it *is* possible."

Out of curiosity, having very little fear of Michael harming the children, I asked Nora, "but what if I feared he was harming them during visits?" I asked.

"You would have to explain your fear to the court, and back it up with proof of some kind," Nora reassured me. "Some people believe it's a good idea tactically to allege impropriety to get a leg up in a custody battle," Nora continued. "but I'd never recommend you do something like that. The courts will punish someone who deliberately lies and harms their children for the sake of a tactical advantage in court. There have been a few cases like that where the mother lost custody due to her unsubstantiated allegations."

"Give me an example," I asked.

"Well, if you falsely alleged that Michael had sexually abused the boys in support of your case for custody and supervised visitation, you would be subject to penalty by the court," Nora answered.

That gave me pause. I could not imagine making false allegations about Michael harming the children. I supposed that was good. Despite his breach of trust, I would never put him through such a horror. Nor would I put the boys through anything so awful.

"You may be interested to know, Sam, that a court could also jail Michael if he refused to pay his support, although it's an extreme penalty that is not often imposed," Nora said.

"Michael is a financial whiz. I've been

reading about the large number of jobs in New York City. Michael has always talked of moving to New York. How would I collect my support if he moved there?" I asked.

"You would reciprocally enforce the support, Sam," Nora explained. "There is reciprocal legislation in effect between most provinces and states that allows you to enforce your Ontario court order in New York, and vice versa."

"So, to summarize, anything Michael and I agree to must be enforceable," I said.

"Exactly, Sam."

# 8

## STEP SEVEN:
## EXPAND YOUR HORIZONS

Separation is a time of change. Both Dr. Morton and Nora kept telling me that. It's a new beginning, even though I never asked for one. Now is the time for me to pursue those activities, life changes and friendships I was not able to pursue during my marriage to Michael. I could learn to play a new instrument, learn a new language, learn to line dance. I could volunteer one day a week with teenage moms and their children. I could start my own art business or art gallery, upgrade my education.

It has been exactly two years since Michael left. Our final separation agreement was signed a few months ago. Kent and Jeff are growing tall and seem to be doing well. I have noticed that Kent has become more independent. His teachers say his confidence has grown. I can only hope that it is due to the way we dealt with the separation. Neither child seems scarred by it and they both still see Michael regularly.

Nora was great. She led me through all of the necessary steps. We had to go to court for spousal support because Michael refused to pay more than $500 a month. I'm now receiving $1200 per month spousal support and $1500 per month child support. I have agreed that my spousal support will end in five years or upon remarriage. I bought the house from Michael in exchange for no equalization payment. Things have been good.

My painting is going well. My sales have increased to $15,000 last year, and another company just called for quotes. My art classes earn about $500 a session and I've been asked to teach at another community centre two miles from home. My ultimate goal is to teach at college or university. I never thought I could teach at all, but now that I am teaching, I figure why not do it at a college or university. As Sandy says, I will probably need to upgrade my credentials over the next three years but once I have, why couldn't I? I've developed an attitude of fearlessness since separation. Why couldn't I start a new relationship? Why couldn't I teach art at college? Why couldn't I lose a bit of weight? Why couldn't I be a single mom and survive? My new attitude has been quite liberating.

Kent is taller than he was, and more confident. He received the Most Valuable Player award on his baseball team, and was named school captain. His marks have been in the mid-70s, and he has taken more responsibility for Jeff over the past 24 months. I have tried to heed Dr. Morton's advice and have not burdened him with caring for his younger brother, although he doesn't seem to mind and the two of them usually get along well. Jeff is still sweet, although he has had problems with depression. I'm taking him to a child psychologist who has seen him five times. I can't tell if it's helping yet. Michael battled me over taking him to a "shrink," telling me the kid wasn't crazy. But I prevailed in the arbitration process set out in our agreement, and I hope the psychologist can help. He seems to be making progress. Jeff is now talking about his feelings more, and watches less television. We will see. He's my sensitive angel, and although I try not to coddle him, I sometimes can't help it. He seems to need me more than Kent. Jeff is more like me; Kent is more like Michael.

I have principal residence of the kids. Michael has them on alternate weekends and every Wednesday night for dinner. We have joint custody. Although it has been difficult, I think it's worth it. Mary Wong was pretty decent, and she helped us mediate a parenting plan that seems to be working. The only hard decision to date was about the child psychologist and I prevailed.

I bought Michael's interest in the home for $66,000, so Michael owed me no equalization payment. I switched banks because mine wouldn't consider my support payments when qualifying for the mortgage and I used a wonderful mortgage broker who obtained a good deal on a mortgage for me.

I have learned a lot about finances and mortgages since Michael left. I read *The Wealthy Barber* three times, and brushed up on my math skills. I'm saving 10 percent of my support income and putting it into mutual funds. I've started a Registered Education Savings Plan for the boys and am contributing $30 per month. I have a mortgage amortized over 25 years at 7 percent. Things have fallen into place. And I actually understand financial stuff. Things I let Michael do because I couldn't be bothered, no longer intimidate me. I can even balance my chequebook.

After all my meetings with Dr. Morton, Mary Wong, and Nora Conway, I am beginning to understand that separation can be an opportunity. I now have the opportunity to pursue activities that I hadn't had time for before. I began reading poetry. I loved Horace's "Carpe diem - seize the day." I had enjoyed poetry before my marriage to Michael. He had always thought it silly and pointless, never understanding the solace I derived from poetry. A few months after he left, I came upon my scribbler from university. A few of my favourite poems were inscribed there.

"How do I love thee? Let me count the ways," wrote Elizabeth Barrett Browning.

Wonderful poem, but not for this time in my life. Although I knew it by heart, I couldn't recite it without crying.

"Happy the man, and happy he alone; he who can call today his own; he who, secure within, can say; tomorrow do they worst, for I have lived today." I loved that poem by Horace. I thought it so apt. Michael's leaving had made me realize how important it was to make every day count.

My favourite, though, was one I'd loved since I was in junior high school. "To whom much is given, much is required." What a great message. Despite all the trauma Michael had put me and the boys through, I had decided I wanted to make life count. To be proud of my accomplishments at the end of the day. To give my all.

Everything I read about separation said to consider it a new beginning. A chance to develop new skills. So in the couple of months after Michael left, I set some goals for myself. This was not my idea; it was Dr. Morton's. "Set three goals for the next year, Sam," he had counseled. It had really helped me focus on the positive, life-changing aspects of separation instead of the negative aspects. So I had set three goals for the next year.

My first goal was to survive the separation. So far, so good.

My second goal was to teach art. I was now

teaching at the Community Centre up the street. I had taken a class there, and got to talking to the activities director about my art. The next thing I knew, I was teaching eight students how to paint. I still can't believe it to this day. I had met a lot of people who were separated and divorced these past two years. On the advice of Sandy, who had been reading dating books, I had joined our Community Centre. I had initially taken a class on the history of the civil war, and remarkably had ended up teaching art there every Tuesday evening.

My third goal was to lose ten pounds. I had not yet accomplished this, and in fact had gained one pound since separation, however next week I intended to begin anew my exercise program. I had struggled with my weight all my life. I had started walking with an acquaintance I had met through my art classes three mornings a week after the boys were in school, and my clothes were fitting better. I would keep at it.

Sandy was at me to upgrade my education to qualify to teach art at college or university. I was considering it. I had picked up the local university continuing education calendar to see what they offered and expected one of these days I would take the plunge. Me teaching at college or university. Who could imagine? I had always dreamed of doing it, but while married I had assumed it would never happen. Now it was potentially within my reach. Amazing what had happened to me since separation.

Sandy and I had also attended a Parents without Partners meeting with the boys and it had been tolerable. I had joined Toastmasters to become more comfortable on my feet while teaching art, and had won the first place ribbon for my first speech. My Toastmasters group was fabulous, and a few of them had been through separation and were good sounding boards.

The boys had learned a few new skills as well. Jeff had begun riding without his training wheels and Kent was a great basketball player. I had purchased a book explaining softball and basketball soon after Michael left, and now was proud to say I understood what was going on, more or less, when I watched my boys play. A small accomplishment, perhaps, but the boys were proud of me and happy I could discuss the games intelligently.

Another acquaintance had just met a new fellow at her fitness club, and she was urging me to join. What I would do at a fitness club was beyond me, however I had promised her I would accompany her in the next couple of weeks. She'd given me a guest pass.

Sandy had also dragged me for a new hairstyle. I had always worn my hair long. Men like long hair. Michael was no exception. What a difference when Maurice cut it all to just below my chin. I looked so different. So much more professional, Sandy said. I wasn't sure, although the boys'' friends' parents complimented me on my new haircut and told me I looked younger. I had become Maurice's regular client. After all, who doesn't want to look younger?

Kent had just started learning French in school, so I decided I would learn with him. We are planning a trip to Quebec City this summer to practice. Kent is much better at it than I am, although I can ask for a bathroom and Sandy taught me a few curse words! I expect we'll survive. Jeff, amazingly, seems to be learning it best of all, and he isn't even studying it. He just picks it up from us and from the television. He is quite a mimic. My angel can imitate Bart Simpson and Beavis and Butthead to perfection. You can imagine our dinner conversations. I never used to understand the term "toilet humour" but having 7 and 11-year-old boys (they were growing up so fast!) I now know the expression was created for them.

The boys are going to horseback riding camp for a week this summer. Sandy is trying to convince me to accompany her to a mountain, but one of my art class participants, Dorothy, recently suggested she and I go to a music camp for the same week to learn a musical instrument. It has been more than twenty years since I last attended camp. What an unusual thought. I have not yet decided.

I have been recording my dreams since separation. One of these days I will ask someone to tell me what they mean. In the meantime, I have been trying to set some ultimate objectives that I want to accomplish in life. So far, I've been uninspired. Or maybe just too busy.

Dr. Morton has told me, now that I have set three short-term goals, to now set three medium-term and long-term goals in the next few months. It sounds so ambitious and exciting. I haven't a clue what I want to accomplish yet.

Before I met Michael, I used to love to sing at the top of my lungs in the car. Obviously when you marry somebody, that is no longer desirable, at least not for the other person. But since separation, I have often been caught at intersections belting out Shania Twain and Celine Dion with my fist as microphone. Some strange looks were the worst of it. I was raised on country music. Michael hated it. So Shania Twain is brilliant in my mind. What an outfit she wore to the Grammys!

I've learned a lot these last twenty-four months. The most important lesson, though, was from Dr. Morton. I am in charge of my own happiness. No one else can make me happy. Slowly but surely, I am making myself happy. They say the best revenge is to live well. I'm learning to live well.

I began by taking stock of where I was and what my skills were. I wrote down that I was a survivor, a great artist, and a great mom. Then I identified the resources in my life that I could count on. Sandy, my mom (she had been a great support to my surprise), my belief in myself and my children.

Then I looked up some old friends that I hadn't seen since marriage. What an uplifting reunion we had. And they knew nothing of Michael so they made me feel young and alive again. I made some new friends through my art classes. They have been fun and full of adventure. I vowed on Dr. Morton's advice to take a few risks and learn a few new skills. That's why I am teaching art. I tried to pamper myself. I began saying 'no' more often. I had my first massage. Finally, and most importantly, time passed. Nora said things would be better in a year or two. Well, they are. Thank God! They couldn't have got much worse.

Dr. Morton had counseled that once I let go of the past and began living in the present, I would make some new friends, start some new hobbies, and grow as a person. He had been right.

Despite society's often damning view of separated families, I had managed to instill in Kent and Jeff self-respect, self-esteem, honesty, integrity, decency, empathy, and personal responsibility. Not half bad for a single mom!

# 9

## STARTING OVER

Starting a new relationship. Learning to love again. I did not initially think it was possible. But my mind was changing slowly.

I am dating again. Remember that neighbour of mine, Rick, who has his children one-week of two? He's nice to me, and he loves to watch me paint. He works for the Transit Commission as an electrician. It's not the same magic as it once was with Michael. I don't know if it will ever be. But I have survived. And he's a caring, considerate companion and, yes, lover.

Dr. Morton had always counseled that I might fall in love again. Maybe I was starting to with Rick. Rick had explained his version of love to me. Unlike Michael, whom I had fallen for passionately and who had never explained his idea of love, Rick had a well thought-out theory. He believed love meant actively empathizing with another, allowing them to be themselves, and enjoying the other's company. It meant being true friends - foul-weather friends - and viewing each other as an equal. Somehow I liked Rick's definition. It was not romantic when written out, but in practice it was really nice. Rick didn't have

Michael's flash, but he also didn't have Michael's roving eye. And a part of me couldn't help but wonder if he wasn't more like my father - always loving me and praising me and hugging me without judgment or criticism.

    Dr. Morton had warned me about rebound relationships. You know, the ones where you hook up with someone to prove you are still lovable. I never took the plunge on a rebound relationship, although I've heard they are very therapeutic. A lot of sex and emotion in a very short period of time, and then you end it. It just wasn't tempting to me.

    I had become more assertive these past two years. I now explained when I felt something was unfair. I had learned not to blame others by using "you did" or "you are" statements, but instead tried to start with "I feel this way because" or "I'm concerned about this because." During my marriage to Michael, I had a tendency to suppress my own needs and only realized after separation that this caused me to resent him and also meant my needs were not met. So, with Rick I was expressing my needs, even when I felt a little uncomfortable. Yet he was appreciative, thanking me for telling him how I was feeling. I believe I deserve happiness. Wow, what a statement!

    Dr. Morton and I had discussed good relationships at length. He counseled me that it is essential that I know myself and be comfortable with myself. If I am incapable of loving myself, I won't be able to love someone else.

He told me that a partner who shares common interests is more likely to be compatible long term and that any relationship I entered should allow me to be my best self. My partner should allow me to grow and develop to be the best I can be, and I should do the same for him. That's the sort of relationship that may last until death do us part.

Nora warned me that to protect the house and the boys' inheritance; I probably needed a prenuptial agreement or marriage contract before marrying again. She explained that with a marriage contract, Rick and I could make our own rules in the event of separation. Although part of me felt that took the trust and spontaneity out of marriage, another part wanted to ensure that Kent and Jeff were protected, so I intended to take Nora's advice. But I will delay that decision until I am ready to remarry, if ever.

Dr. Morton and I discussed at length dating, and the children's reactions to my dating, before Rick and I went out. He told me that a lot of parents asked their children's permission to date again. He said that was inappropriate. He told me instead to sit down calmly with the boys and explain that mommy would be making friendships over the next little while, and that I still loved them.

It seemed to work.

Dr. Morton also related that a lot of parents gave their children too much detail about the date and the sexual activity occurring. I had been surprised at that, thinking I was never one to discuss sexual activity with Michael or Sandy let alone the children. Rick and I had taken it slow and hadn't had sexual relations until the children were on a sleep over at a friends one evening after we had been dating for four months. Given what I had been through, I really appreciated that.

Before Rick, I went on two blind dates. They were awful. Steve had preached the entire evening and tried to convert me to his religion on our first date. Curtis had been the opposite, a slime ball. He had his hand on my knee at dinner and was moving up when I stood up, told him I had to go to the washroom, and walked out the door. Yech!

On the other hand, Rick had been great. Fun loving, great with the boys - although initially they had been extremely unkind to him, probably seeing him as a rival to their father. Rick had persevered, telling them he liked them and that he hoped in time they would also like him, and they had warmed up.

Rick and I had discussed marriage. He told me he was ready anytime I was. I appreciated his honesty and devotion. I just wasn't quite ready for marriage again. Dr. Morton and I had discussed stepfamilies. He told me they were difficult but rewarding. I could only imagine. Adjusting to life without Michael had been tough on the boys. I assumed another change so soon would be even more difficult. Kent and Jeff would probably be all right, I figured, but I expected they would not accept being disciplined by Rick. I suppose we could work that out in time. Dr. Morton had warned me not to force the boys to call Rick "dad" but to let them call him Rick and respect their feelings. So far they had been pretty well adjusted with him.

    Michael told me last week he wants a divorce. One last difficult step. He has long since moved on from Jennifer, and seems to have a new partner every few months. He seems empty inside when I see him. Maybe I just want him to seem empty. I wonder if he ever wonders, in the middle of the night, like I sometimes do, what I'm doing and why we are not together again. I've often fantasized that he was with me again, that we were making love. I always wake up feeling a bit uneasy when that happens, although Dr. Morton has assured me it's normal to have all sorts of dreams about your ex-spouse.

    Michael had hit the roof when he found out I was dating again. To this day he refuses to talk to Rick when he is there at access exchange. He called me a slut, a whore, and threatened to take the children away from me. Although initially guilty and shaken by his comments, I calmed down once I spoke with Nora, who reassured me I was entitled to date and remarry. I sort of knew that, but it was good to hear it from Nora. She reiterated that as long as the children were not in danger or subject to harm, no court would take them away from me. Michael had eventually calmed down somewhat. When I told Sandy, she became outraged, telling me that he had a lot of nerve becoming angry with me, given Jennifer and the string of other women he kept around. I didn't become outraged. Somehow I found it a compliment that he was still jealous. He had never treated women's sexual activity the same as men's, preferring to believe men were different and needed to conquer women, whereas women should be family-focussed. In my sessions with Dr. Morton, I had realized that women and men both need to be loved, and that there was nothing wrong with my new relationship; in fact, there was a lot right about it. Dr. Morton said Michael would accept it in time.

Given the terms of our separation agreement, I have teased with Sandy I will wait to marry Rick until five years are up to maximize Michael's financial pain. We will see.

When I asked Nora about divorce, she advised that it was extremely straightforward since we had completed our separation agreement. She said it would take from two to four months and only involved paperwork. No necessary court appearances, no nasty affidavits. Just $1000 or so and it would be over, and I would be free to remarry. She also asked about the necessary Catholic annulment. I told her I had spoken with the priest just last week who assured me it would not be difficult. And it sounded like Michael was going to pay for the divorce.

It still hurts when I see Michael. There is still a connection there that I doubt will ever go away. I sometimes wonder whether I would take him back if he showed up on my doorstep and begged. Sandy tells me I wouldn't. I'll have to take her word for it because I don't know.

Rick has two girls, 13 and 15. They both mother Jeff, which he seems to enjoy, and tease Kent, which he equally enjoys. I can't quite picture all of us living together in some sort of Brady Bunch utopia, but perhaps as the months pass I will be able to visualize us as one family.

All in all, things have turned out okay. Nora was right. It just takes time. Well, I'm off to Kent's softball game. Rick and the girls are accompanying me. Jeff is at a friend's sleep over party.

Best of luck to all of you. Above all, remember, in time everything will work out.

## APPENDIX A: RESOURCES

Academy of Family Mediators
5 Militia Drive
Lexington, MA  02421
(781)674-2663
Fax:  (781) 674-2690
e-mail:  afmoffice@mediators.org
http://www.mediators.org

American Academy of Child and Adolescent Psychiatry
3615 Wisconsin Ave. N.W.
Washington, DC  20016-3007
(202) 966-7300
Fax:  (202) 966-2891
e-mail:  mbell@aacap.org
http://www.aacap.org

American Bar Association (ABA)
750 North Lake Shore Drive
Chicago, IL  60611
(312) 988-5000
email:  info@abanet.org
http://www.abanet.org

American Divorce Association of Men (ADAM)
1519 South Arlington Heights Road
Arlington Heights, IL  60005
(847) 364-1555
Fax:  (847) 364-7273

American Psychiatric Association
Division of Public Affairs
1400 K Street, N.W.
Washington, DC  20005
(202) 682-6000
Fax:  (202) 682-6114
e-mail:  apa@psych.org
http://www.psych.org

American Psychological Association
750 First Street, N.E.
Washington, DC  20002
(202) 336-5700
http://www.apa.org

Association for Children for Enforcement of Support Inc.
2260 Upton Avenue
Toledo, OH  43606
(800) 738-ACES
Fax:  (419) 472-6295
email:  ACES@childsupport-ACES.org
http://www.childsupport-aces.org/

Canadian Bar Association
902-50 O'Connor Street
Ottawa, ON K1P 6L2
(613) 237-2925
1-800-267-8860
Fax: (613) 237-0185
email: info@cba.org
www.cba.org

Canadian Lawyer Index
1604-60 Pleasant Blvd.
Toronto, ON M4T 1K1
(416) 923-8578
Fax: (416) 923-8458
info@canlaw.com
www.canlaw.com

Children's Rights Counsel
Suite 401
300 I Street N.E.
Washington, DC 20002
(202) 547-6227
(800) 787-kids
Fax: (202) 546-4272
e-mail: crcdc@erols.com
http://www.vix.com/crc/

Joint Custody Association
10606 Wilkins Avenue
Los Angeles, CA 90024
(310) 475-5352
Fax: (310) 475.6541

National Alliance for the Mentally Ill (NAMI)
200 North Glebe Road, No. 1015
Arlington, VA 22203-3754
(800) 950-nami
Fax: (703) 524-9094
http://www.nami.org/

National Coalition Against Domestic Violence
P.O. Box 18749
Denver, CO 80218
(303) 839-1852
Fax: (303) 831-9251

National Mental Health Association
1021 Prince Street
Alexandria, VA 22314-2971
(703) 684-7722
(800) 969-nmha
Fax: (703) 684-5968
http://www.nmha.org

National Organization of Women (NOW)
1000 16th Street NW
Suite 700
Washington, D.C. 20036
(202) 331-0066
Fax: (202) 785-8576
email: now@now.org
www.now.org

New Directions
542 Mount Pleasant Road
Toronto, ON M4S 2M7
(416) 487-5317?

North American Conference of Separated and Divorced Catholics
P.O. Box 360
Richland, OR 97870
(541) 893-6089
Fax: (541) 893-6089*51
e-mail: nacsdc@pdx.oneworld.com
http://www.eoni.com/nacsdc

Parents, Families, and Friends of Lesbians and Gays
1101 14th Street, N.W.
Suite 1030
Washington, DC 20005
(202) 638-4200
Fax: (202) 638-0243
e-mail: info@pflag.org
http://www.pflag.org
Parents Without Partners Inc.
401 N. Michigan Avenue
Chicago, Illinois 60611-4267
(312) 644-6610
(800) 637-7974
http://www.parentswithoutpartners.org

Stepfamily Association of America
650 J Street
Suite 205
Lincoln, NE 68508
(800) 735-0329
Fax: (402) 477-8317
e-mail: stepfamfs@aol.com
http://www.stepfam.org

Stepfamily Foundation Inc.
333 West End Avenue
New York, NY 10023
(212) 877-3244
Fax: (212) 362-7030
e-mail: staff@stepfamily.org
http://www.stepfamily.org/

# APPENDIX B:
# NORTH AMERICAN LAW SOCIETIES & BAR ASSOCIATIONS

United States:

Alabama State Bar Association
(334) 269-1515
(334) 261-6310
www.alabar.org

Alaska State Bar Association
(907) 272-7469
(907) 272-2932
www.alaskabar.org

Arizona State Bar Association
(602) 252-4804
(602) 271-4930
www.azbar.org

Arkansas State Bar Association
(501) 375-4606
(501) 375-4901
www.arkbar.com

California State Bar Association
(415) 561-8200
(415) 561-8892
www.calbar.org

Colorado State Bar Association
(303) 860-1115
(303) 894-0821
www.cobar.org

Conneticut State Bar Association
(860) 721-0025
(860) 257-4125
www.ctbar.org

Delaware State Bar Association
(302) 658-5279
(302) 658-5212
www.dsba.org

District of Columbia State Bar Association
(202) 737-4700
(202) 626-3471
www.dcbar.org

Florida State Bar Association
(850) 561-5600
(850) 561-5827
www.flabar.org

Georgia State Bar Association
(404) 527-8700
(404) 527-8717
www.gabar.org

Hawaii State Bar Association
(808) 537-1868
(808) 521-7936
www.hsba.org

Idaho State Bar Association
(208) 334-4500
(208) 334-4515
www.state.id.us.isb

Illinois State Bar Association
(217) 525-1760
(217) 525-0712
www.illinoisbar.org

Indiana State Bar Association
(317) 639-5465
(317) 266-2588
www.isbaadmin&nibar.org

Iowa State Bar Association
(515) 243-3179
(515) 243-2511
www.iowabar.org

Kansas State Bar Association
(785) 234-5696
(785) 234-3813
www.kansbar.org

Kentucky State Bar Association
(502) 564-3795
(502) 564-3225
www.kybar.org

Louisiana State Bar Association
(504) 566-1600
(504) 566-0930
www.lsba.org

Maine State Bar Association
(207) 622-7523
(207) 623-0083
www.maineba.org

Maryland State Bar Association
(410) 685-7878
(410) 837-0518
www.msba.org

Massachusetts State Bar Association
(617) 338-0500
(617) 338-0650
www.masbar.org

Michigan State Bar Association
(517) 346-6327
(517) 372-2410
www.michbar.org

Minnesota State Bar Association
(612) 333-1183
(612) 333-4927
www.mnbar.org

Mississippi State Bar Association
(601) 948-4471
(601) 355-8635
www.msbar.org

Missouri State Bar Association
(573) 635-4128
(573) 635-2811
www.mobar.org

Montana State Bar Association
(406) 442-7660
(406) 442-7763
www.montanabar.org

Nebraska State Bar Association
(402) 475-7091
(402) 475-7098
www.nebar.com

Nevada State Bar Association
(702) 382-2200
(702) 385-2878
www.nvbar.org

New Hampshire State Bar Association
(603) 224-6942
(603) 224-2910
www.nhbar.org

New Jersey State Bar Association
(732) 249-5000
(732) 249-2815

New Mexico State Bar Association
(505) 797-6099
(505) 828-3765
www.nmbar.org

New York State Bar Association
(518) 463-3200
(518) 463-4276
www.nysba.org

North Carolina State Bar Association
(919) 828-4620
(919) 821-9168
www.ncbar.com

North Dakota State Bar Association
(701) 255-1404
(701) 224-1621

Ohio State Bar Association
(614) 487-2050
(614) 487-1008
www.ohiobar.org

Oklahoma State Bar Association
(405) 524-2365
(405) 416-7001
www.okbar.org

Oregon State Bar Association
(503) 620-0222
(503) 684-1366
www.lsbar.org

Pennsylvania State Bar Association
(717) 238-6715
(717) 238-1204
www.pabar.org

Rhode Island State Bar Association
(401) 421-5740
(401) 421-2703
www.ribar.com

South Carolina State Bar Association
(803) 799-6653
(803) 799-4118
www.scbar.org

South Dakota State Bar Association
(605) 224-7554
(605) 224-0282
www.sdbar.org

Tennessee State Bar Association
(615) 383-7421
(615) 297-8058
www.tba.org

Texas State Bar Association
(512) 463-1463
(512) 463-1475
www.texasbar.com

Utah State Bar Association
(801) 531-9077
(801) 531-0660
www.utahbar.org

Vermont State Bar Association
(802) 223-2020
(802) 223-1573
www.vtbar.org

Virginia State Bar Association
(804) 644-0041
(804) 644-0052
www.vba.org

Washington State Bar Association
(206) 727-8200
(206) 727-8320
www.wsba.org

West Virginia State Bar Association
(304) 558-2456
(304) 558-2467
www.wvbar.org

Wisconsin State Bar Association
(608) 257-3838
(608) 257- 5502
www.wisbar.org

Wyoming State Bar Association
(307) 632-9061
(307) 632-3737
www.wyomingbar.org

## Canada:

Law Society of Alberta
(403) 229-4700
(403) 228-1728
www.lawsocietyalberta.com

Law Society of British Columbia
(604) 669-2533
(604) 669-5232
www.lawsociey.bc.ca

Law Society of Manitoba
(204) 942-5571
(204) 956-0624
www.lawsociety.mb.ca

Law Society of New Brunswick
(506) 458-8540
(506) 451-1421

Law Society of Newfoundland
(709) 722-4740
(709) 722-8902

Law Society of the Northwest Territories
(867) 873-3828
(867) 873-6344
www.lawsociety.nt.ca

Law Society of Nova Scotia
(902) 422-1491
(902) 429-4869
www.nsbf.nf.ca

Law Society of Prince Edward Island
(902) 566-1666
(902) 368-7557

Law Society of Quebec
(514) 954-3438
(514) 954-3478
www.baroeau.qc.ca

Law Society of Saskatchewan
(306) 569-8242
(306) 352-2989
www.lawsociety.sk.ca

Law Society of Upper Canada
(416) 947-3300
(416) 947-5967
www.lsuc.on.ca

Law Society of the Yukon
(867) 668-4231
(867) 667-7556

# APPENDIX C:
# SAMPLE FINANCIAL STATEMENT AND BUDGET

**INCOME:**

All sources of income:

Income/Salary:
Interest income:
Social assistance:
Pensions:
Unemployment insurance:
Rent:
Support:

Benefits through employment:

Medical and dental coverage:
Pension:
Life and disability insurance:
Car allowance:

Total Income:

## EXPENSES:

Housing

Rent
Real property taxes
Mortgage
Common expense charges
Water
Electricity
Natural gas
Fuel oil
Telephone
Cable T.V.
Home Insurance
Repairs and maintenance
Gardening and snow removal
Other (Specify)

Food, Toiletries and Sundries

Groceries
Meals outside home
Grooming
General household supplies
Laundry, dry cleaning
Other (Specify)

## Clothing

Children
Self

## Transportation

Public transit
Taxis, car pools
Car Insurance
Licence
Car maintenance
Gasoline, oil
Parking
Other (Specify)

## Health and Medical

Doctors, chiropractors
Dentist (regular care)
Orthodontist or special dental care
Insurance premiums
Drugs
Other (Specify)

## Deductions from Income

Income tax
Federal Pension Plan
Unemployment insurance
Employer pension
Union or other dues
Group insurance
Credit union loan
Credit union savings
Other (Specify)

## Miscellaneous

Life insurance premiums
Tuition fees, books, etc.
Entertainment
Recreation
Vacation
Gifts
Babysitting, day care
Children's allowances
Children's activities
Support payments
Newspapers, periodicals
Alcohol, tobacco
Charities
Income tax (not deducted at source)
Other (Specify)

Loan Payments

Banks
Finance companies
Credit unions
Department stores
Other (Specify)

Savings

R.R.S.P.
Other (Specify)

Total Expenses:

**ASSETS:**

Land:
General household contents
Jewelry
Cars, boats, vehicles
Savings and Savings Plans
Pension Plans
Securities
Life and Disability Insurance
Accounts Receivable
Business interests
Other property

Total Assets:

Debts

Property owned on date of marriage

Property gifted from third parties

Property disposed of in the past three years

Name and address of employer

Copy of last income tax return

## APPENDIX D:
## INFORMATION YOUR LAWYER WILL WANT TO KNOW

Name:
Address:

Date of birth:
Place of birth:
Phone number:
Where are you working:
Earnings:
Business number:

Spouse's name:
Spouse's address:

Spouse's date of birth:
Spouse's place of birth:
Spouse's place of employment:
Spouse's earnings:

Date you began dating:
Date of cohabitation:
Date of marriage:
Date of separation:

Children's names:
Dates of birth:
School or daycare and cost:

Reason for the separation:

Your goals:

Surname at birth:
Surname before marriage:
Spouse's Surname at birth:
Spouse's Surname before marriage:

Norma Walton conducts seminars and workshops on *The Seven Steps to a Successful Separation* and other topics.

For information, or to book her for your organization or company, please contact:

Global Perspectives Inc.
820 Mount Pleasant Road
Toronto, Canada  M4P 2L2
Tel: (416) 489-6448
or 1-800-771-0322
Fax: (416) 489-9973

Could someone you know benefit from reading *The Seven Steps to a Successful Separation: Common Sense Tips to Surviving the Breakdown of your Relationship?* It's the perfect gift for anyone going through a separation - understandable, enjoyable and helpful.